'Til

HEAVEN INVADES EARTH

'Til

HEAVEN INVADES EARTH

CINDY TRIMM

CHARISMA
HOUSE

Most CHARISMA HOUSE BOOK GROUP products are available at special quantity discounts for bulk purchase for sales promotions, premiums, fund-raising, and educational needs. For details, write Charisma House Book Group, 600 Rinehart Road, Lake Mary, Florida 32746, or telephone (407) 333-0600.

'TIL HEAVEN INVADES EARTH by Cindy Trimm
Published by Charisma House
Charisma Media/Charisma House Book Group
600 Rinehart Road
Lake Mary, Florida 32746
www.charismahouse.com

Scripture quotations marked THE MESSAGE are from *The Message: The Bible in Contemporary English*, copyright © 1993, 1994, 1995, 1996, 2000, 2001, 2002. Used by permission of NavPress Publishing Group.

Cover design by Justin Evans
Design Director: Bill Johnson
Manuscript Preparation: Rick Killian, www.killiancreative.com

Visit the author's website at www.trimminternational.org

Library of Congress Cataloging-in-Publication Data:
An application to register this book for cataloging has been submitted to the Library of Congress.
International Standard Book Number: 978-1-62136-290-6
E-book ISBN: 978-1-62136-291-3

While the author has made every effort to provide accurate telephone numbers and Internet addresses at the time of publication, neither the publisher nor the author assumes any responsibility for errors or for changes that occur after publication.

First edition

13 14 15 16 17 — 9 8 7 6 5 4 3 2 1
Printed in the United States of America

CONTENTS

The people of the land have used oppressions, committed robbery, and mistreated the poor and needy; and they wrongfully oppress the stranger. So I sought for a man among them who would make a wall, and stand in the gap before Me on behalf of the land, that I should not destroy it; but I found no one.

—Ezekiel 22:29–30

Then the King will say... "Enter, you who are blessed by my Father! Take what's coming to you in this kingdom. It's been ready for you since the world's foundation. And here's why:

I was hungry and you fed me,
I was thirsty and you gave me a drink,
I was homeless and you gave me a room,
I was shivering and you gave me clothes,
I was sick and you stopped to visit,
I was in prison and you came to me."

Then those "sheep" are going to say, "Master, what are you talking about? When did we ever see you hungry and feed you, thirsty and give you a drink? And when did we ever see you sick or in prison and come to you?" Then the King will say, "I'm telling the solemn truth: Whenever you did one of these things to someone overlooked or ignored, that was me—you did it to me."

—Matthew 25:34–40,
The Message

PROLOGUE

*Let us therefore come boldly to the throne
of grace, that we may obtain mercy and
find grace to help in time of need.*

HEBREWS 4:16

A S SHE STOOD at the threshold of the inner court that day, she knew she was one step away from death.

To enter the presence of the king without being summoned was viewed as the equivalent of an assassination attempt. To do so was to be executed on sight, save that the king had favor on you and extended his scepter, signifying his sovereign permission for you to come before him and make a petition.

Esther knew full well the danger of what she was doing that day—but even more, she knew if she didn't, her people were marked for genocide. Someone had to stand up. Someone had to speak out. Someone had to go to the king and ask for justice—even if they didn't survive the attempt.

But Esther was no fool either. She would not come into the throne room rashly, making demands or shouting protests. She was not going to intimidate the king into seeing things her way. What she needed to do was present her case with wisdom and decorum.

So, first, she prepared herself for the audience, fasting for three days and nights before she would step before the king. She was not alone in preparing for this critical audience. Many others, including her cousin, her closest relative, joined her in praying and fasting from wherever they were.

As the time approached, she considered carefully what she would wear and how she would adorn herself—clothing herself in the finest robes and applying the cosmetics and perfume she knew His Royal Highness would like best. After all, she was the king's bride. She was intimately familiar with what pleased him most and what disturbed him the most deeply. She knew how he administered justice, the inequities and discriminations that touched his heart, and the things that pleased him most. She knew, in the end, it wasn't about what she wanted. It was about what he wanted, what he would allow, and what he couldn't stand to see happen. It was about asking him to step in to use his sovereignty to right what was wrong despite whatever other jurisdictions or authorities stood in those places.

She also knew it would demand patience. The king was not one to be rushed or do something according to any other timetable but his own. So, if he extended the scepter to her, she would not make her request there, but she would invite him to dine with her, not once, even, but twice, before she would make her entreaty. She would lavish her attention and love on the king first, before even thinking of asking for anything, letting him know it was not what he could do that she cherished, but who he was to her.

Then, lastly, she wouldn't ask only for deliverance, but she would also ask for the empowering of the people about to face attack. Rescue is wonderful, but strength to fend for and defend oneself was even better. She wouldn't ask for a solution that would indebt them to someone else, but for the power to resolve the challenges they were about to face for themselves. She would ask that they be given the arms they needed to defeat the foes about to oppose them. Their deliverance would be by their own hands through the blessing of the king.

With her strategy in place, dressed as the royal bride, Esther stepped from the comfort of her own quarters into the presence of the king. One way or the other, she knew it would cost her everything—it was justice or death. But as her cousin had queried, "Who knows whether you have not attained royalty for such a time as this?" (Esther 4:14, NAS).

INTRODUCTION

*They seek Me day by day and delight to know
My ways.... They ask Me for just decisions,
they delight in the nearness of God.*

Isaiah 58:2, nas

I CAN THINK OF few better pictures of intercession than the story of Esther. She stood, in a foreign land, before her king, for the sake of her people. By doing so, she literally placed her life on the line for the benefit of others. As Jesus described such resolve, "Greater love has no one than this, than to lay down one's life for his friends" (John 15:13). Though we go before a far more just King than Esther did, I think there is much to learn about the anatomy of intercessory prayer from the picture of Esther standing before the throne of judgment. There is much we can take from her attitude and preparation that will make our prayers for others more effective.

Intercessory prayer is a call of duty for every Christian on our planet. Like military service, it demands training, sacrifice, and discipline. That is not to say that it is a life without joy—far from it, in fact—but it is a duty that is challenging enough that few really dare to embrace it as we should. It is often a lonely endeavor that gets us little recognition from anywhere but heaven, and therefore almost anything else in our lives will distract us from it unless we are sincerely determined. As Christian practices go, we love church attendance, praise and worship, Bible studies, missions' trips, hearing special speakers, attending conferences, weekend retreats, Bible studies, and even weekly prayer meetings. There is no question that gathering together is a great way to take some of the difficulty out of the practice of prayer. However, an hour or two a week really doesn't cut it. If you don't believe me, just look at the world around us today. Things are the way they are because no one is standing before the throne of heaven to ask that it be otherwise. "The kingdom of heaven suffers violence, and the violent take it by force" (Matt. 11:12). Where are our prayer warriors who will violently oppose the violence being done to the vulnerable and innocent in every community, city, and nation around the earth?

This verse isn't talking about starting a revolution or rioting in the streets demanding change. We know change can be won that way—just look at the Middle East after the Arab Spring—but those nations are now suffering from governments just as oppressive and corrupt, if not more so, than what they had before. They enforced change, but it was neither lasting change nor change for the better. No, this speaks of a people who will go boldly into the throne room of heaven with a relentless do-or-die attitude like the one Esther had. We "lay down our lives" not so much by being willing to die, but by being what saints of the past called "living martyrs." There are people who live according to the protocols of heaven rather than living trapped by the temptations of the earth. No, these people don't all live in monasteries or nunneries, nor are they all on the mission field living in a mud hut, nor or they all working in a church. Though I have the greatest respect for people who do all of these things—who gather in weekly prayer meetings in order to be the "praying heart of the church," or who risk their lives taking the gospel of Jesus Christ to the farthest reaches of the planet—not all of us are called to that kind of life, though I do believe all of us are called to intercession.

What do I mean by that? What I mean is that living martyrs look like anyone else you might see walking down the street of any town or city, but rather than living by the dictates of their workplaces and consumer culture, they live by the heartbeat of heaven. They are great workers, and they often have nice things, but their nice things don't have them. Their activities during their free hours are not dictated by the television schedule, what's on at the movies, where the sales are, or seasonal sports events. Sure, they may enjoy those things, but these people put first things first, living by the principle of Matthew 6:33: "Seek first the kingdom of God and His righteousness, and all these things shall be added to you." They are all about the priorities of the kingdom of God before the pleasures of this world. They enjoy life according to God's guidelines and dictates—and they certainly aren't shy about sacrificing an hour or two a day of their "me" time to lay themselves before God and ask for the empowerment of others that they might be able to overcome whatever it is they are facing. The apostle Paul described it this way:

For I consider that the sufferings of this present time are not worthy to be compared with the glory that is to be revealed to us. For the anxious longing of the creation waits eagerly for the revealing of the sons [and daughters] of God. For the creation was subjected to futility, not willingly, but because of Him who subjected it, in hope that the creation itself also will be set free from its slavery to corruption into the freedom of the glory of the children of God. For we know that the whole creation groans and suffers the pains of childbirth together until now....

In the same way the Spirit also helps our weakness; for we do not know how to pray as we should, but the Spirit Himself intercedes for us with groanings too deep for words; and He who searches the hearts knows what the mind of the Spirit is, because *He intercedes for the saints according to the will of God.* And we know that God causes all things to work together for good to those who love God, to those who are called according to His purpose.

—Romans 8:18–22, 26–28, nas,

emphasis added

What Paul is saying here is that the earth itself groans because of the corruption that has come with a fallen world—sin has consequences. Our planet and our bodies weren't designed to endure it. Sin corrupts or exploits almost everything it touches, and it is a two-edged blade—while it's true that he who lives by the sword (sin) dies by the sword (sin), before he does, he will cut a lot of other people first. This is the justice that intercessors violently demand—that evil be confronted as it was when Jesus confronted Paul on the road to Damascus. It must be stopped, but hearts must also be transformed.

What will save our planet? *The manifestation of the sons and daughters of God.* When we become the children of God who we are each called to be—plugged into and led by the Holy Spirit, maturing into the fully functioning tripartite beings we were designed to become—things will change for the better. The kingdom of God *will* be manifest—not on the whole earth at first, perhaps, but at least in those places where we have influence. We must come into agreement with the prayers and burdens God Himself carries for our world. And who is it that knows what the mind of God is regarding every problem facing the world today? "He [the Holy Spirit] intercedes for the saints according to the will of God" (Rom. 8:27, nas).

Intercessory prayer is not all about correctly wording our petitions so that they persuade a passive God into action. God is a proactive God—He isn't sitting on His hands waiting for someone to talk Him into doing good on the earth. However, at the same time He has decreed that every individual has the right to exercise free will. He is not going to violate His own word to intervene on the earth or even in a person's life. He wants the best for all of us, but each of us must first invite Him in so that He can do that work of grace. The same is true for the earth. God must be invited in to manifest His kingdom in whatever areas we touch.

God knows what our needs are before we even ask, even when we pray for others. Thus intercession is not just about pleading a cause and getting answers. We don't just get answers to our prayers—*we become answers*. We gain knowledge and insight into solutions. We become aware of ministries or organizations that address the same issues we are praying for, and we empower them. We grow in determination and strength to see our battles through to the end. Our hearts become knit together with God's heart to establish His desires upon the earth—His blessings, His divine healing, His ways, His wisdom, His kingdom. At the same time we grow and touch the lives of others, infecting them with the sense of purpose and mission with which God has infected us.

The underlying purpose of all prayer is to become our authentic selves. We do that by putting aside life's distractions and daily demands to spend time with God getting His plan for our lives, His plan for how we can impact our communities, and His plan for how we might heal the nations of our world. It is about presenting the issues of the world to the Father and letting Him teach us how to be part of the solution. It is about taking our places as children of God to stand up for not only the human beings who don't know Him yet and those brothers and sisters in need of His blessings in their lives, but also the oppressed, the hungry, the enslaved, the exploited, the poor, and the underprivileged. If we are truly going to make a difference concerning such issues, we don't need more "good" ideas—we need God answers.

Andrew Murray described intercession this way in his book *With Christ in the School of Prayer*:

It is in intercession that the Church is to find and wield its highest power, that each member of the Church is to prove his descent from Israel [Jacob], who as a prince had power with God and with men, and prevailed....

I feel sure that as long as we look on prayer chiefly as the means of maintaining our own Christian life, we shall not know fully what it is meant to be. But when we learn to regard it as the highest part of the work entrusted to us, the root and strength of all other work, we shall see that there is nothing that we so need to study and practice as the art of praying aright....It is only when the Church gives herself up to this holy work of intercession that we can expect the power of Christ to manifest itself in her behalf.[1]

If this is true—and I believe that it is—there is no true, lasting change that happens upon the earth that is not birthed out of prayer. And because of this, there is no Christian activity that the devil fights harder, or our flesh will resist with more distractions, than true, intimate intercession. When we step before our King, we know He will extend His scepter to demonstrate His favor upon us, but we are not just there for ourselves. This isn't a game. There is a time to come before the throne of God just to be with Him—to climb into the lap of our "Daddy." But there are also times when the princes and princesses of God come before the Father with formal requests as emissaries of those who cannot or will not speak for themselves. Esther was the queen, the wife of King Ahasuerus, yet that day she did not come as a wife to a husband but as an ambassador to a king. It didn't change their intimate relationship, but what it did was say, "I know we know each other, but at the same time, I am willing to risk the relationship—to risk death itself—to come before you today on behalf of someone else." As Paul prayed:

> For I could wish that I myself were accursed from Christ for my brethren, my countrymen according to the flesh, who are Israelites, to whom pertain the adoption, the glory, the covenants, the giving of the law, the service of God, and the promises; of whom are the fathers and from whom, according to the flesh, Christ came, who is over all, the eternally blessed God. Amen.
>
> —Romans 9:3–5

No, Paul did not become separated from Christ because of his longing to see the people of Israel come to know Him as he did. But he was willing to put himself on the line. He was willing to test his relationship with God by asking for a hard thing—something far more than just "God bless me and my loved ones."

We, the body of Christ on the earth, must understand intercessory prayer and must intercede for the nations if we are to have the impact upon the earth that God has called us to have. We must transform ourselves into more than just "Christians." We must become the children of God He specifically intended us to be. We must become our authentic selves. We must be willing to lay down this world for the sake of those who need Him—even those who make themselves our enemies.

We live in what can be considered the greatest age of the earth. We are closer to Christ's return than any other generation before us. What will He catch us in the middle of when He returns? Will we be praying, walking out the plans He gave us when we were in prayer, working on some world-changing invention or program, or simply sitting on our talents buried deep in the ground because we were complacent or afraid?

I can't speak for you, but I know what I will be doing!

> Who then is a faithful and wise servant, whom his master made ruler over his household, to give them food in due season? Blessed is that servant whom his master, when he comes, will find so doing. Assuredly, I say to you that he will make him ruler over all his goods. But if that evil servant says in his heart, "My master is delaying his coming," and begins to beat his fellow servants, and to eat and drink with the drunkards, the master of that servant will come on a day when he is not looking for him and at an hour that he is not aware of, and will cut him in two and appoint him his portion with the hypocrites. There shall be weeping and gnashing of teeth.
> —Matthew 24:45–51

PART ONE

THE COURT OF HEAVEN

The bedrock of our Christian faith is the unmerited, fathomless marvel of the love of God exhibited on the Cross of Calvary, a love we never can and never shall merit. Paul says this is the reason we are more than conquerors in all these things, super-victors, with a joy we would not have but for the very things which look as if they are going to overwhelm us....

When we pray on the ground of Redemption, God creates something He can create in no other way than through intercessory prayer.[1]

OSWALD CHAMBERS

The one concern of the devil is to keep Christians from praying. He fears nothing from prayer-less studies, prayer-less work, and prayer-less religion. He laughs at our toil, mocks at our wisdom, but trembles when we pray.[2]

SAMUEL CHADWICK

ONE

ADVOCACY BEFORE
THE THRONE

Understanding the Judiciary of Heaven

*Put Me in remembrance, let us argue our case together;
state your cause, that you may be proved right.*

ISAIAH 43:26, NAS

*It is also of the greatest importance for
the soul to go to prayer with courage.*[1]

MADAME JEANNE GUYON

O NE OF THE most famous pictures of
the twentieth century was that of the
"Unknown Rebel"—often referred to
as "Tank Man"—who stood defiantly in front of a

column of Chinese Type 59 tanks the day after the brutal clearing of student protestors from Tiananmen Square on June 4, 1989. You have probably seen the picture; if not, simply searching for "Tank Man" on the Internet will bring up several versions of it, and even some video. According to official channels, no one ever found out who this man was or what ever happened to him. For many the picture became a symbol of the power of nonviolent protest. One ordinary man, carrying what looked to be his groceries, standing resolutely in front of a column of tanks, any one of which could easily roll over him, but because of the humanity of the lead tank driver, rather than rolling over him, the entire column stood at a standstill. When the man cut off the attempts of the tanks to drive around him, he moved back to stand before the lead tank again, and the column was forced again to a halt. It was as if the courage of that one man was able to stop the entire Chinese Army. Had only this been the case the day before—if only someone had been able to stand between the army and stop them on that day—then the thousands of causalities that resulted from that crackdown would have been spared.

The cornerstone scripture on intercession paints

a very similar picture. I like how *The Message* para-phrases it:

> Extortion is rife, robbery is epidemic, the poor and needy are abused, outsiders are kicked around at will, with no access to justice.
>
> I looked for someone to stand up for me against all this, to repair the defenses of the city, to take a stand for me and stand in the gap to protect this land so I wouldn't have to destroy it. I couldn't find anyone. Not one.
>
> —Ezekiel 22:29–30, The Message

Sounds a lot like the age we live in, doesn't it?

If you were to look back through history, corrup-tion like this only changed with times of great soci-etal awakening. Israel saw it under praying kings like David, Hezekiah, and Josiah. The Great Awakening of the 1700s was birthed in the 24/7 prayer of the Moravians at Herrnhut and in the methodical devotion of John and Charles Wesley and George Whitefield. Typical of his attitude about prayer, John Wesley once said, "I pray two hours every morning. That is if I don't have a lot to do. If I have a lot to do that day, then I pray three hours." The Second Great Awakening was grounded in prayer as well, especially from intercessors like Daniel Nash and Abel Clary, who were pivotal to the success of Charles Finney's ministry. Of "Father" Nash, Finney would later write:

> I have seen Christians who would be in an agony [of prayer], when the minister was going into the pulpit, for fear his mind should be in a cloud, or his heart cold, or he should have no unction, and so a blessing should not come. I have labored with a man of this sort. He would pray until he got an assurance in his mind that God would be with me in preaching, and sometimes he would pray himself ill. I have known the time when he has been in darkness for a season, while the people were gathering, and his mind was full of anxiety, and he would go again and again to pray, till finally he would come into the room with a placid face, and say, "The Lord has come, and he will be with us." And I do not know that I ever found him mistaken.[2]

With Daniel Nash going before him into each town to pray before Finney arrived there to preach, Finney's ministry reached its height in Rochester, New York, in 1830. The entire community transformed because of its excitement about knowing God. Businesses closed when church meetings were being held because there would be no one around to shop. Bars and theaters closed because of the lack of patronage—former patrons chose instead to attend prayer meetings or Bible studies. Crime rates plummeted and charitable work flourished. Though Rochester was home to only about ten thousand people at the time, one hundred thousand were added to churches in the city and surrounding area. Where we are lucky today to see 20 percent of the converts stay faithful to church attendance after a revival meeting, more than 80 percent of those who made decision to follow Jesus during Finney's meetings pursued God for the rest of their lives.[3]

Many also contrast what happened in England during the Great Awakening and what happened in France during the same period. With economic, social, and governmental problems being quite similar, England saw a great revival and France a bloody revolution. It's easy to feel like you are accomplishing nothing when you bow your knee to pray for others, but the truth is, there is no greater power on earth than someone who will kneel in prayer with the resolve of that unknown rebel standing before those tanks. To stand in the spirit between evil and those it would crush is how the kingdom of God changes the world around us. It was at the center of William Wilberforce's work to end slavery in the British Empire. It was at the center of George Washington Carver's inventive genius to deliver southern share-croppers from absolute poverty. It was at the cornerstone of the civil rights movement. It is one thing to stand in nonviolent protest and march against oppression, but only when that resolve is mixed with prayer do societies actually transform.

Just think of any organization or ministry that has touched the world for good, and you will see prayer at the foundation of it. The Salvation Army of the late 1800s grew from a single mission in London to having posts around the world in a mere two or three decades because the Salvationists practiced "knee drills"—prayer meetings—with military discipline. When General William Booth once received word that an overseas post was struggling to establish itself, he responded with a simple two-word telegram: "Try tears." When the Salvationists there took the attitude of pleading for the people of the nation who were suffering to their prayer meetings, things began to change dramatically.[4]

There is a level of praise and prayer that is deeply beneficial to us as individuals. It keeps us on the path God has called us to and helps us experience the blessings and success that God wants for us. This kind of prayer is wonderful and indispensable in our lives. In it we do from time to time pray for others— especially our loved ones, friends, and coworkers— the people who touch our lives. We will lay our petitions at the foot of the cross on their behalf. This is intercession, and it is wonderful, but it is not the level of intercession I am talking about. I am talking about a regular, systematic, strategic defense on behalf of individuals or entire people groups suffering from the forces of darkness. I am talking about a prepared, enduring, unswerving determination to see freedom won for people we may never meet. It is not about individual requests for individual people— though that will happen in the process. It is about laying down your life for a period of time (hours, days, weekends, perhaps) to call on heaven to invade earth. It is to lay siege to institutions of darkness— poverty, slavery, oppression, hunger, crime, drug abuse, domestic violence, war, access to clean water, widowhood and orphaned hearts, divorce, you name it—and plead for deliverance in the court of heaven.

The Right Type of Prayer
for the Right Time

In his book *The Art of Prayer* Kenneth Hagin delineates several different kinds of prayer mentioned in the Scriptures and states:

> The most effective prayer is the prayer the Holy Spirit inspires *which is needed at the moment*—whether it is the prayer of agreement, the prayer of faith, the prayer of praise and worship, or some other type of prayer. Often different kinds of prayer will work together much like the fingers on a hand.[5]

Such different types of prayer have a tendency to overlap, synchronize, and synergize, yet at the same time it is helpful to be able to identify each and understand their unique purpose and parameters. This isn't to be legalistic or dogmatic, nor is it something you will use in your prayers along the lines of saying, "Now, Lord, I want to go over my prayers of petition." But as the Spirit of God leads and guides you in prayer, it helps to understand what something is and what it isn't, and when it is time to make our requests and when it is time to be grateful for their answers, even if they haven't manifested in the natural world yet.

So rather than delineating each specific type of prayer mentioned in the Bible, let's think of them is some overarching categories. Here are the main ones I think we should consider as they are used in or with intercession:

1. Petitions and supplications

2. Consecration and dedication (or what I like to call "release" prayers)

3. The prayer of agreement

4. Praise, worship, thanksgiving

Intercession itself is really any prayer that we pray for others, or more distinctly, it is any prayer where we go before the throne of God on behalf of another who cannot go on behalf of himself for reasons of not knowing God, not being in right relationship with Him, or not understanding his rightful place in prayer before the Father. In *The Art of Prayer* Kenneth Hagin defined intercession as "standing in the gap in prayer between a person or persons, who have provoked judgment upon themselves through their wrongdoing, and the actual execution of that judgment."[6] Prayer general Cindy Jacobs describes it this way: "True intercession is actually twofold. One aspect is asking God for divine intervention; the other is destroying the works of Satan."[7] Dick Eastman of Every Home for Christ described it this way: "An intercessor is a man or woman—or child—who fights on behalf of others. As such, intercession is the activity that identifies us most with Christ. To be an intercessor is to be like Jesus because that is what Jesus is like. He ever lives to intercede."[8] In other words, the person who intercedes is the person who steps in front of the tank of coming calamity to stop it before it runs over someone we care about—even if it is someone we have never met. And because faith works through love, as we see in Galatians 5:6, love has to be involved for whomever we pray.

I would add to these definitions that intercession can also be made on behalf of the innocent who are facing calamity for no action of their own. Thus we have the right to stand in prayer for the unborn who are threatened by abortion, children who suffer domestic violence and other forms of abuse, those kidnapped and trafficked in the sex trade industry, or others like them.

When we come to God on their behalves, we come with heartfelt and earnest supplications, or individual requests for specific things that we humbly submit to God. To make a supplication is like presenting a petition to a governing body, expressing the will of the people signing it for action or intervention. This doesn't mean we have to go out and get a bunch of signatures, for as many have said, "One plus God equals a majority." We are, in essence, praying "the prayer of agreement" according to Matthew 18:19–20 with God Himself rather than another person.

> If two of you agree on earth concerning anything that they ask, it will be done for them by My Father in heaven. For where two or three are gathered together in My name, I am there in the midst of them.

One of the things about making a petition or supplication is that just as when we come before a human governing body, the more specific and well defined our request, the better it will be received. Vague prayers have a way of receiving vague answers, or at least answers that we are not sure were specifically given to what we prayed for because, honestly, we didn't pray for anything specifically.

Before I go more into that point, let me next touch on the prayers of consecration and dedication, for they have similar issues involved. The prayer of consecration is usually the prayer of an individual setting himself apart from his own personal desires to accept the will of God for his life. It is a "Yes, Lord" prayer, and it is best exemplified by Jesus's prayer in the Garden of Gethsemane:

> [Jesus] said to the disciples, "Sit here while I go and pray over there." And He took with Him Peter and the two sons of Zebedee, and He began to be sorrowful and deeply distressed. Then He said to them, "My soul is exceedingly sorrowful, even to death. Stay here and watch with Me." He went a little farther and fell on His face, and prayed, saying, "O My Father, if it is possible, let this cup pass from Me; nevertheless, not as I will, but as You will."
> —MATTHEW 26:36–39

In the prayer of consecration the individual is giving up his or her own will to accept the will and plan of God.

Akin to this is the prayer of dedication, in which we are dedicating or releasing something into God's hands and out of our own. We are in essence saying, "God, I am not going to worry or fret any more about this issue. I am giving it to You. I am leaving it at the foot of Your throne. I am not going to touch it again in my thought life except to praise and thank You that it is in Your hands and is taken care of." It is praying according to 1 Peter 5:7: "Casting all your care upon Him, for He cares for you." This is a prayer best done for the people closest to us whom we have such a tendency to fret over and worry about to the point that we get in the way of our own prayers being answered because fear and worry have a way of eating away at the faith we have that things will ever change for them.

What I want you to see about prayers of petition and supplications as well as the prayer of consecration and dedication is that they are specific in nature, and they discern the will of God in the situations for which they are being prayed. Too many think that intercession is simply adding names to the end of your prayers before bedtime as we did as children, "…and Lord, bless Aunt Hattie and Uncle Reuben. Bless Mommy and Daddy, and my sisters and brothers too. Please take care of all of the orphans in Africa and the people who are hungry. Amen." While that is a good place to start, we need to spend enough time in intercession to allow God to direct us in the specifics of what we should be petitioning heaven to be done for each of these people or groups.

Neither is it simply praying, "Lord, Thy will be done," as if that were as proper a closing to prayer as "Amen"—as if by praying that we have covered anything we might have missed that we should have mentioned. The only time that phrase is used in prayer is by Jesus in His prayer of consecration to the Father's will of going to the cross. It was prayed with Jesus knowing full well what the will of God was. In order for us to pray, "Thy will be done," we have to know what that will is as well.

Thus intercession is not just prayer for others; it is spending time with God (in prayer and studying His Word) to learn His will for those for whom we are praying and then lifting that will back up to God as a petition or supplication. It is the sense in which we "contend together" (Isa. 43:26) with God in presenting our intercessions before the court of heaven.

Once we lay our prayers before the Father, praise, worship, and thanksgiving take over. Though sometimes, depending on the prayer and how specific the things are that we are praying for, we will bring the same matters before God again and again like the persistent widow before the unjust judge (Luke 18:2–8), most things we will pray for once and then simply praise and thank God that they are taken care of from then on out. (This in essence is the prayer of faith: to pray for something and believe it is taken care of at that moment.) In a prayer of dedication, we are laying our concern at His feet and then trust God to take it from there. The more specific our prayers, the more we can trust God for specific answers. Once we perceive in the spirit that they have been taken care of in heaven, we have but to thank God and praise Him for their manifestations upon the earth. For larger matters (like those we will discuss in chapter 6), we will come to God for more incremental and strategic supplications that we will learn over time and will develop with Him. All of this is prayer in the Spirit working together with God as we intercede. It is the divine partnership He desires.

After all, His asking us to pray that His will be done on the earth as it is in heaven is not just a matter of semantics—it is a legal precedent for how God designated authority over our world and our lives.

You Have Jurisdiction

John Wesley once said, "God does nothing but in answer to prayer....Every new victory which a soul gains is the effect of a new prayer."[9] I believe this is because one way to look at intercession is in terms of presenting a case before a court. A lot of people emphasize the sovereignty of God—and there is no question that our King is sovereign—but they seem to forget what David said prophetically about God: "You have magnified Your word above all Your name" (Ps. 138:2). If there is one thing that trumps the sovereignty of God, it is His faithfulness. God is not a liar. By His very nature, if there is one thing He holds above His ability to do anything on the earth, it is the promises He has made and the authority He has given.

In the very first chapter of the Bible we are told that after creating the earth, the Father, the Son, and the Holy Spirit had a conversation together, saying:

> Let Us make man in Our image, according to Our likeness; let them *have dominion* over the fish of the sea, over the birds of the air,

and over the cattle, over all the earth and over
every creeping thing that creeps on the earth.
—GENESIS 1:26,
EMPHASIS ADDED

This tells us that God gave *dominion*—or
jurisdiction—of the earth over to humanity. He said,
"This is yours. You take care of it. I will give you a
handbook for doing that later on, but for now, let's
walk and talk together in the cool of each day and
talk over what you are going to do with this planet
I have given you. If you need help, just ask, but it is
yours to manage and prosper as you see fit."

Now, let's explore this a little bit. I have several
friends who have teenage children who have turned
sixteen and gotten their licenses. Suppose those parents said, "Honey, I am so proud of you. You have
earned the right to drive, your grades are good, you
are growing into a responsible adult, and you have
saved up some money from your summer job to get a
car. Well, we have decided that instead of you buying
your own car, we are going to buy one for you. It will
be your car though. You will need to take care of it.
You will need to buy your own gas and pay for its

maintenance. You will have to buy the insurance for it. But we are giving it to you. It's yours."

Now, if those parents were really giving their child that car, would it really be the son's or daughter's car if they never let them drive it? If they said, "We'll put it in the garage and you can look at it any time you want—it's yours after all—but we'll hang onto the keys. Cars are dangerous after all. You could hurt yourself or someone else, so we will hang onto it. If you need to go somewhere, we will be glad to drive you. But it's your car! Enjoy it!"

That young person might own the car and even have his or her name on the registration, but does he have *dominion* over the car? No, of course not. The parents are still in control. The parents are making the decisions. In essence, they haven't really given the child the car at all. It is still the parent's car.

But that is not what God did. He gave humanity the dominion over the earth and therefore declared the earth humanity's jurisdiction. He said, "Look! I made all of this, and it is Mine to give, so I am giving it to you and putting you in charge. It is yours to do with as you would like. It is yours to care for and nurture. And you know what? Because it is yours, I am not going to step in to do things unless I am asked.

That is what *dominion* means, after all. It means I am giving you the authority over it. I won't step in to do anything on your turf unless you ask Me, or unless I absolutely have to intervene for your sake or the sake of the entire planet—and it will have to be a real emergency for Me to step in like that. You have *My word*."

This is oversimplified, but the church must realize that although God is the ultimate, sovereign authority, He has given us responsibility for our lives and our world. He has given us ownership and free will—the power to choose what to do with what He has given us. With that authority comes responsibility. The choices we make stand. They have eternal consequences. We have what we have today because of choices that were made. Our children and their children will be impacted by the choices you and I make—whether we choose to act, or not to act, to pray or not to pray. We must embrace the responsibility we've been given. God is bound by His own word not to intervene every time we act irresponsibly—or even unresponsively. If He stepped in and changed things every time we made a bad decision, or no decision at all, then He wouldn't have really given us dominion, would He?

The problem is, it didn't take Adam and Eve long to fumble their authority and give it over to Satan by disobeying God. God had given them one commandment to keep in order to hang onto their authority, and Satan tricked them into violating their lease.

And there was another issue. The earthly ecosystem was built on obedience and doing what was right, not on disobedience and wrong choices. The earth prospered and gave life when righteousness was done, but it suffered under sin. Sin brought corruption. The earth groaned and warped under sin. The very atmosphere itself changed.

Some Christian scientists have suggested that at Creation the earth was wrapped in a layer of water vapor high in the stratosphere that would have caused the entire earth to be somewhat of a giant greenhouse, causing temperatures to be uniform throughout the earth no matter the season. It would have meant no Weather Channel would have ever been needed—every day would be "sunny with a high of seventy-two degrees," even at the poles. This moist atmosphere would have been a tropical paradise, plants needing nothing but the moisture that was already in the air to water them.

However, because sin threatened to choke the

earth to death, this water canopy "tore," resulting in the great Flood. It was the first time anyone had ever seen rain, let alone storms and the hurricane-force winds that must have resulted from the rapid changes in temperatures. These scientists hold that once that canopy of water vapor broke, the poles would have frozen in seconds, causing the animals there to instantly freeze, as it is believed to have happened to the woolly mammoth found frozen whole in Siberia. Weather has never been the same after the Flood, ushering in everything from gentle snows to hurricanes. The earth's crust began to shift and buckle, causing earthquakes and tsunamis. These I believe to be the futility and groans Paul spoke of in Romans 8:

> For the creation was subjected to futility, not willingly, but because of Him who subjected it in hope; because the creation itself also will be delivered from the bondage of corruption into the glorious liberty of the children of God. For we know that the whole creation groans and labors with birth pangs together until now.
> —ROMANS 8:20–22

The only answer at that time for sin was retribution: "...life for life, eye for eye, tooth for tooth, hand for hand, foot for foot, burn for burn, wound for wound, stripe for stripe" (Exod. 21:23–25). This is where the system of animal sacrifice came in—sin required death, and since the life of a creature is in the blood, blood had to be shed to cover sin: "For the life of the flesh is in the blood, and I have given it to you upon the altar to make atonement for your souls; for it is the blood that makes atonement for the soul" (Lev. 17:11). It was a messy business, indeed.

But Jesus Christ changed all of that. Through His own blood He paid the price of sin once and for all, with one caveat. Free will still reigned. He refused to take back the jurisdiction He had given to humanity through Adam and Eve. Though our sin is paid for through the blood and grace of Jesus Christ, if we don't accept His sacrifice on our behalf, it doesn't do us or our planet any good. Jesus gave His life for us and demands that we give up our sinful, selfish lives for Him. It is only by doing so that we enter into the kingdom of God as it was intended from the beginning. We are asked to give up our sinful life so God can fill us with His eternal life, as Scripture says:

This is how much God loved the world: He
gave his Son, his one and only Son. And this
is why: so that no one need be destroyed; by
believing in him, anyone can have a whole and
lasting life. God didn't go to all the trouble of
sending his Son merely to point an accusing
finger, telling the world how bad it was. He
came to help, to put the world right again.
Anyone who trusts in him is acquitted; anyone
who refuses to trust him has long since been
under the death sentence without knowing it.
And why? Because of that person's failure to
believe in the one-of-a-kind Son of God when
introduced to him.

—John 3:16–18, The Message

When Adam and Eve sinned, they lost their jurisdiction over the things of the earth to Satan, or more
correctly stated, perhaps, to sin. Where sin reigned,
Satan, the enemy of our souls, the adversary, had his
way. As Paul explained it, "Just as through one man
[Adam] sin entered the world, and death through sin,
and thus death spread to all men, because all sinned"
(Rom. 5:12). However, he went on to say in the following verses:

> (For if by the one man's offense death reigned through the one, much more those who receive abundance of grace and of the gift of righteousness will reign in life through the One, Jesus Christ.) Therefore, as through one man's offense judgment came to all men, resulting in condemnation, even so through one Man's righteous act the free gift came to all men, resulting in justification of life. For as by one man's disobedience many were made sinners, so also by one Man's obedience many will be made righteous.
>
> —ROMANS 5:17–19

God could not change the rules He had set up at the beginning without violating His own word; however, above that word was His law. He had the legal right to step in sovereignly because His law allowed Him to do so without violating His word or His promises. Thus Jesus came and gave the keys of the kingdom back to humanity through those who would "believe in the one-of-a-kind Son of God when introduced to him" (John 3:18, THE MESSAGE). The earth thus groans for the manifestation of the sons and daughters of God because that is its salvation! When we become who God designed and called us to be, kingdoms shift—the upside-down world gets turned right side up!

However, having legal jurisdiction means nothing if it is not enforced. While we are truly in charge, Satan runs around with forged documents, lying to everyone, saying he still is. He acts *like* a tough guy—a roaring lion. "Your adversary the devil walks about *like* a roaring lion, seeking whom he may devour" (1 Pet. 5:8, emphasis added). But while he acts *like* it, he, in fact, is *no* lion, and he is *not* in charge of anything on the earth. We have but to resist him and he will be forced to flee (v. 9). That is why his main tools are deception, ignorance, and misunderstanding. He can only get his way by tricking others into exercising their authority to do what he wants. Sadly he is very successful at this.

Why? Because far too few stand up before the throne of heaven and call him out as an imposter and a fake. We acquiesce our authority and jurisdiction because it is either inconvenient to pray that much, we have been fooled ourselves about our true power and authority, we are trapped in the traditions of men into empty expressions of our religion and callings, or we don't know the "law of God"—the Bible— His holy handbook to us and His final word on every matter that needs to be decided. We then become as useless as a lawyer who doesn't know the law.

Legal systems in the Western world, however, are based on the patterns of the Bible for deciding justice and issuing fair sentences. As best as we have been able to do, we have tried to imitate in our courtrooms what happens before the judgment throne of God. Because of that we can look to our legal systems as one model for interceding for others. Charles Finney trained as a lawyer before he became a preacher, and that training was crucial to his revivals. He would argue the case for people's salvation before them as if he were an advocate and they were the jury who had to decide their own cases. I am sure he did the same in prayer, taking a boldness based in the knowledge of the Bible to God to argue with such conviction for the souls of others that he even sometimes surprised himself with demands so insistent he wondered that he wasn't being overly confident or even bordering on being disrespectful. As he described it:

> I found myself so much exercised, and so borne down with the weight of immortal souls, that I was constrained to pray without ceasing. Some of my experiences, indeed,

alarmed me. A spirit of importunity some-times came upon me so that I would say to God that he had made a promise to answer prayer, and I could not, and would not, be denied. I felt so certain that he would hear me, and that faithfulness to his promises, and to himself, rendered it impossible that he should not hear and answer, that frequently I found myself saying to him, "I hope thou dost not think that I can be denied. I come with thy faithful promises in my hand, and I cannot be denied." I cannot tell how absurd unbelief looked to me, and how certain it was, in my mind, that God would answer prayer—those prayers that, from day to day, and from hour to hour, I found myself offering in such agony and faith. I had no idea of the shape the answer would take, the locality in which the prayers would be answered, or the exact time of the answer. My impression was that the answer was near, even at the door.[10]

This, my friends, is what intercession is all about. It is pleading for others in the court of heaven based on the very laws and Word God has given us to argue before Him and call for His kingdom to manifest upon the earth. It is a call of duty for every Christian, and it is our right as children of the King. He will not step in where He is not invited, and even then He must be invited in such a way that there is no doubt, no second guessing, no wavering.

Brothers and sisters, it is time for us to stand up in the court of heaven for the peoples of this earth—especially for those who don't yet know how to stand up for themselves. But if we are to successfully argue our cases, we have to know the law—we have to take God at His Word and grab His promises with both hands.

It's time for us to go to law school.

Two

THE KING WE SERVE

Inside Information on the Supreme Judge

*You can count on it. From now on, whatever you
request along the lines of who I am and what
I am doing, I'll do it. That's how the Father
will be seen for who he is in the Son. I mean
it. Whatever you request in this way, I'll do.*

JOHN 14:12–14, THE MESSAGE

The root of faith is the knowledge of a Person.[1]

OSWALD CHAMBERS

EVERY LEGAL SYSTEM is based on the authority of its government and the rule of law. The kingdom of heaven is no different. However, if the rulers of the government are corrupt, things will go differently. Law will be perverted and corrupted. There are also jurisdiction issues—you don't go to the DMV if your house has been broken into, you don't request a building permit from the state legislature, and you don't call the IRS to suggest a new law. Every branch, bureau, agency, and administration has its responsibilities, jurisdiction, and limitations. In essence, we can't expect government officials to do what they haven't been designated to do. As it is with human beings, we are lucky to get politicians to do what they promised when they were elected, let alone go the extra mile for us. There are always forms to be filled out and bureaucracy to be navigated to get what is rightfully ours. If you don't know the system, chances are you will never get even what is designated for you.

While the kingdom of heaven is certainly different, James tells us that, "You do not have because you do not ask. You ask and do not receive, because you ask amiss" (James 4:2–3). *Amiss* here means in the wrong way or with the wrong motives. Selfish desires based on our own lusts—to indulge ourselves or corrupt our natures—don't even get a hearing in heaven. It is not in the nature of God to give us things that will destroy us in the short or long run. His nature is to bless, not to curse, as James 1:17 tells us: "Every good gift and every perfect gift is from above, and comes down from the Father of lights, with whom there is no variation or shadow of turning." There are no "mixed blessings" with God.

However, at the same time, many don't even ask in the first place because they have been deceived about who God really is. They are afraid of Him or they only see the extreme justice side of Him. ("God's justice" is another issue that we will discuss in more detail in another chapter—it is not what most people think it is.) Like the steward who hid his talent, they think, "Lord, I knew you to be a hard man, reaping where you have not sown, and gathering where you have not scattered seed. And I was afraid, and went and hid your talent in the ground" (Matt. 25:24–25). Rather than investing their time in prayer to address the things that tear at their hearts, they bury their hurts in the ground and hide their heads in the sand, ignoring what is happening on the nightly news— things we should be inviting God to do something about.

But this is not how Jesus taught us to pray, nor is it who God revealed Himself to be in the Scriptures. Even in the Old Testament God was not just about judgment. He revealed Himself to be very different. In fact, He gave Israel names to call Him that represented who He wanted to be to them.

God Most High

> "Blessed be Abram of God Most High, possessor of heaven and earth; and blessed be God Most High, who has delivered your enemies into your hand." And he gave him a tithe of all.
> —Genesis 14:19–20

> And he [the demon] cried out with a loud voice and said, "What have I to do with You, Jesus, Son of the Most High God? I implore You by God that You do not torment me."
> —Mark 5:7

The Hebrew term for "God Most High" is *El Elyon*, which first appears in this passage in Genesis 14. The story here is quite noteworthy, and I believe it gives a good picture of where this name of God comes from.

In a battle in the Valley of Siddim the armies of Sodom and Gomorrah retreated before a stronger foe, leaving their camp and goods. The valley was filled with asphalt pits, and many fell into them in their flight; some were captured. Among the captured was Lot, Abram's nephew, who was living in Sodom at that time and thus part of its army. When Abram heard that his nephew had been taken captive, he mounted a rescue mission. As a result, he rescued not only Lot and his goods but also the other captives and the goods of the kings of Sodom and Gomorrah.

Returning from this victory, Abram is met by one of the most mysterious figures in the pages of the Bible: Melchizedek, king of Salem, and the priest of God Most High. Melchizedek meets Abram with bread and wine, the elements of the covenant meal that Jesus commemorated at the Last Supper and that we use to remember Him in Communion. It is a sacramental part of God's cutting of covenant with Abram (also known as a "testament"—thus the "Old Testament" of this covenant with Abram and the "New Testament" of our covenant with God through Jesus Christ are reflected in this). Who exactly Melchizedek was is not revealed anywhere else in Genesis. In fact, this is the only mention of him in the entire Bible except for a brief reference in Psalm 110 and in Hebrews 5 and 6 where the writer quotes Psalm 110 and speaks of Jesus as being "High Priest 'according to the order of Melchizedek'" (Heb. 5:10). Some even believe that Melchizedek is Jesus manifesting Himself to Abraham as representative of the covenant He would one day cut in His own blood. (This is also the first place in the Bible that the tithe is mentioned as Abraham tithes to Melchizedek of all the spoils he took in the battle.)

Melchizedek is priest of "God Most High," of *El Elyon*, and meets Abram so that Abram might acknowledge that the strength with which he defeated this army was God's, not his own. Melchizedek calls him "Abram of God Most High" so that he would know it was God, the God above all other gods and King above all other kings, who won the victory for him that day—a victory that Abram and his servants won but the allied forces of five kings could not.

This name tells us that there is no power, principality, authority, or "god" that is greater than the God of Abraham, Isaac, and Jacob. Through the king of Salem, or *shalom*, "peace," God proclaims His might to Abram, and Abram bows to that strength, tithing to His priest and partaking in the covenant meal with His representative. In it God lets us know, "There is no one like the LORD our God" (Exod. 8:10).

GOD ALMIGHTY

> When Abram was ninety-nine years old, the
> LORD appeared to Abram and said to him, "I
> am Almighty God; walk before Me and be
> blameless."
> —GENESIS 17:1

> "I am the Alpha and the Omega, the Beginning
> and the End," says the Lord, "who is and who
> was and who is to come, the Almighty."
> —REVELATION 1:8

A few chapters later God appears to Abraham
again and announces Himself as *El Shaddai*, "God
Almighty." In this case, however, God is not only
declaring Himself above all other gods, and thus able
to defeat them and those who follow them, but He is
also announcing that He is the God of creation and
above creation's natural laws. Where Abram's wife,
Sarai, has been barren, God will bring forth a son
for Abram, that Abram's line would continue. He is
not just God Most High; He is also God Almighty—
there is nothing He does not have the power to do
or to change.

The Everlasting God

> Then Abraham planted a tamarisk tree in Beersheba, and there called on the name of the Lord, the Everlasting God.
>
> —Genesis 21:33

> Jesus Christ is the same yesterday, today, and forever.
>
> —Hebrews 13:8

In Genesis 21 we meet God as the Eternal and Everlasting One: *El Olam*, God Everlasting. He is the God who does not change, who has always been and will always be. It is the precursor to the name *Jehovah*, "I AM," the God who is in every moment past, present, and future—the God who sees all, knows all, and can do whatever He sees fit to do without limitation.

The Lord's Provision Shall Be Seen

> And Abraham called the name of the place, The-Lord-Will-Provide; as it is said to this day, "In the Mount of The Lord it shall be provided."
>
> —Genesis 22:14

> God is able to make all grace abound toward
> you, that you, always having all sufficiency in
> all things, may have an abundance for every
> good work.
> —2 CORINTHIANS 9:8

And as if power and authority weren't enough, God goes on to tell us what He is to us in more specific terms. The next is in Genesis 22, as part of the story of God calling Abraham to sacrifice his heir, Isaac, on the mountaintop. Abraham takes Isaac to the mountaintop believing that even if he has to go so far as to kill Isaac, "God was able to raise him up, even from the dead" (Heb. 11:19) if necessary to keep His promise that "through Isaac your descendants shall be named" (Gen. 21:12, NAS). However, instead of bringing Isaac back to life, God stays Abraham's hand and shows him a ram caught in a thicket to be used as an offering instead.

At that instant Abraham looks to heaven and calls that place by the name God inspires in him at that moment: *Jehovah Jireh*, "The God Who Provides," or as many paraphrase it, "God My Provider." In the midst of the wilderness, when Abraham had a need, God provided it for him. Is there any reason to think God is any less of a provider today?

GOD HEALS

> If you diligently heed the voice of the LORD
> your God and do what is right in His sight,
> give ear to His commandments and keep all
> His statutes, I will put none of the diseases on
> you which I have brought on the Egyptians.
> For I am the LORD who heals you.
>
> —EXODUS 15:26

> Who Himself bore our sins in His own body
> on the tree, that we, having died to sins, might
> live for righteousness—by whose stripes you
> were healed.
>
> —1 PETER 2:24

Exodus 15:26 declares God to be *Jehovah Rophe*,
"The God Who Heals Us." God does not put disease on His children to teach them things. That is
ludicrous! He is a loving Father. If there was a father
who was a doctor and had access to petri dishes of
the polio virus, what would you think of him if he
used that virus on his son because the boy would
never sit down and do his homework? You would
think he was a monster, wouldn't you? Not a loving
father! Well, if that is true, then the same goes for our

heavenly Father. We live in enemy territory where disease is a weapon the enemy uses to open fire upon humanity. Certainly God can teach and strengthen you through your sickness, but He is not the inflictor of illness any more than a physician would make you sick in order for you to seek treatment.

Certainly sickness and disease are in the world today because of sin, and sometimes disease comes as a direct result of our sin—smoking leads to lung cancer, promiscuity can lead to sexually transmitted infections, gluttony is directly connected to heart disease, and worry can contribute to high blood pressure—but other times illness takes hold regardless of our choices or whether or not we "deserve" it. Take, for example, the man born blind whom Jesus is asked about in John 9:2: "Rabbi, who sinned, this man or his parents, that he was born blind?" Jesus's answer?

> Neither this man nor his parents sinned, but that the works of God should be revealed in him. I must work the works of Him who sent Me while it is day; the night is coming when no one can work. As long as I am in the world, I am the light of the world.
>
> —John 9:3–5

In other words, his blindness wasn't the direct result of sin—and I do not believe Jesus was saying he was born blind just so that He could come by one day and heal him, to the glory of God. I think the punctuation is in the wrong place. (In the original Greek they didn't use punctuation; modern translators inserted periods and commas to make it easier to read.) This passage reads very differently if you put a period after "sinned" instead of a comma and then a comma after the word "him" at the end of that sentence. It would then read: "Neither this man nor his parents sinned. But that the works of God should be revealed in him, I must work the works of Him who sent Me." Jesus isn't concerned with cause and effect here—because there isn't any—but He is concerned with healing! God is not the one who puts diseases on people, but when we come to Him in faith, abiding in His Spirit and His Word abiding in us, then He is *Jehovah Rophe*, "The God Who Heals Us."

GOD MY BANNER

Moses built an altar and called its name, The-Lord-Is-My-Banner; for he said, "Because

the LORD has sworn: the LORD will have war
with Amalek from generation to generation."
—EXODUS 17:15–16

Thanks be to God, who gives us the victory
through our Lord Jesus Christ.
—1 CORINTHIANS 15:57

When troops marched into battle in these ancient times, the army would always carry the banners—or today, the flags—of the nation and the units before each division. It signified who they were and what they stood for. They didn't stand for a piece of cloth, but that piece of cloth represented who they were as a people. Banners tell a story—the colors, stripes, stars, or other emblems all have meanings. They are so important that we remember great moments of carrying our flags into battle, like the monument of the raising of the flag at Iwo Jima during World War II, or we remember the scene from the movie *Glory* when Denzel Washington picks up the Union flag after the bearer drops it and rallies the troops to renew their assault on Fort Wagner.

Jehovah Nissi, "The Lord Is My Banner," signifies the battle we have against evil on this earth and that doing good is our mission in the name of Jesus

Christ—this is our battle cry. In the days of The Salvation Army they marched under a banner displaying the words "Blood and Fire," symbolizing that they were going to triumph by the blood of Jesus and the fire of the Holy Spirit.

As we face the problems of our day and intercede for those who can't or don't know how to pray for themselves, we need to remember the banner under which we approach the throne—the very name of God Himself.

The Lord Who Sanctifies

> Speak also to the children of Israel, saying: "Surely My Sabbaths you shall keep, for it is a sign between Me and you throughout your generations, that you may know that I am the LORD who sanctifies you."
>
> —Exodus 31:13

> Therefore do not be ashamed of the testimony of our Lord, nor of me His prisoner, but share with me in the sufferings for the gospel according to the power of God, who has saved us and called us with a holy calling, not according to our works, but according to

His own purpose and grace which was given
to us in Christ Jesus before time began.
—2 TIMOTHY 1:8–9

For centuries and even today the Hebrew people
have been set aside from the rest of the world by
their observance of the Sabbath—the period starting
at sundown on Friday evening and ending at sundown on Saturday. It was a time to rest, yes, but it
also began with a ceremony of blessing during which
the parents, particularly the father, spoke a blessing
over his children.

I recently heard a story of an up-and-coming
young woman in a law firm who, no matter what was
happening or the workload that needed to be done
before the following week, left work a little early
on Friday afternoon. This woman was a go-getter
and very polished and polite, so it was a surprise to
her colleagues as they pondered big issues that she
would simply pack up and leave, even in the middle
of important Friday afternoon meetings. One day
one of her coworkers asked her about this practice.
She answered, "I have to leave early because I have to
drive two hours to my parents' house for our Sabbath
meal." "Are you that religious?" the other asked. "Oh,

it is not about religion. I don't go out of duty. I go to hear my father speak his blessings over me. Every Friday night he takes me in his arms and speaks his blessings over me for that week. I can't go without those. I would not be the person I am today without hearing those blessings spoken over me each week."

The word *sanctification* signifies a "setting apart of something for a special purpose." It denotes separating something out as special. The Greek word for "church" is *ecclesia*, which means, "the called-out ones." We have been called out of the troubles and limitations of the world to be used for good, as catalysts of positive change, and as a people looking to establish the city of God on the earth. "The God Who Sanctifies," *Jehovah M'kaddesh*, is the God who has called us out of the chaos of the world system to manifest His grace and transformational power.

THE LORD IS PEACE

> So Gideon built an altar there to the LORD, and called it The-Lord-Is-Peace.
>
> —JUDGES 6:24

> Be anxious for nothing, but in everything by prayer and supplication, with thanksgiving,

let your requests be made known to God; and the peace of God, which surpasses all understanding, will guard your hearts and minds through Christ Jesus.

—Philippians 4:6–7

Jehovah Shalom, "The Lord Is Peace," is our surety in time of trouble or conflict. Many think of peace treaties when they think of the word *peace:* an agreement to cease fire and end hostilities between different groups. However, the Hebrew word shalom means much more. According to *Vine's Complete Expository Dictionary of Old and New Testament Words, shalom* represents a:

> …relationship…of harmony and wholeness, which is the opposite of the state of strife and war….Shalom as a harmonious state of the soul and mind encourages the development of the faculties and powers. The state of being at ease is experienced both externally and internally….Shalom also signifies "peace," indicative of a prosperous relationship between two or more parties.[2]

It is not just a peace where there is an absence of open conflict, but *shalom* is also a relationship of genuine good will and brotherly love toward the other party. It is an attitude of being sneaky in trying to bless the other, no matter what. It is another word that is indispensable in discussing the attitudes of one toward another in covenant relationships. Would only that more of our marriages were based on this kind of peace rather than simply nonconfrontational coexistence!

The Lord of Hosts

> This man went up from his city yearly to worship and sacrifice to the Lord of hosts in Shiloh.
> —1 Samuel 1:3

> Or do you think that I cannot now pray to My Father, and He will provide Me with more than twelve legions of angels?
> —Matthew 26:53

Jehovah Sabaoth, or "The Lord of Hosts," signifies the legions of angels God has at His disposal to do His will. Unlike the devil, with whom a third of the angels fell when they followed him, God is a creator—so if He needs more angels, He can always create them, while Satan has no such power. In other words, if God needs to send an angel to perform a certain task in response to your prayers, He will never lack the "staff" to get the job done.

THE LORD MY SHEPHERD

The LORD is my shepherd;
I shall not want.
He makes me to lie down in green pastures;
He leads me beside the still waters.
He restores my soul;
He leads me in the paths of righteousness
For His name's sake.
Yea, though I walk through the valley of the
shadow of death,
I will fear no evil;
For You are with me;
Your rod and Your staff, they comfort me.
You prepare a table before me in the presence
of my enemies;
You anoint my head with oil;
My cup runs over.
Surely goodness and mercy shall follow me
All the days of my life;

And I will dwell in the house of the Lord
Forever.

—Psalm 23:1–6

When he brings out his own sheep, he goes
before them; and the sheep follow him, for
they know his voice.

—John 10:4

David's picture in Psalm 23 of "The Lord My
Shepherd"—*Jehovah Rohi*—is one of the most poignant in Scripture. It represents the God who guides
you and leads you to green pastures, still waters, and
out the other side of the valley of the shadow of
death. He arranges things so that your enemies hold
banquets in your honor, anoints you with His Holy
Spirit, and sends goodness and mercy in hot pursuit
of you. Through prayer you get to know His voice and
thus His guidance. As Oswald Chambers described
it: "When you are rightly related to God, it is a life of
freedom and liberty and delight, you *are* God's will,
and all your commonsense decisions are His will for
you unless He checks."[3] It is a radical relationship
with God that only comes through friendship with
God at the level of Abraham, Moses, David, or Paul—
all individuals dedicated to intercessory prayer.

GOD OUR RIGHTEOUSNESS

In His days Judah will be saved,
And Israel will dwell safely;
Now this is His name by which He will be
      called:
THE LORD OUR RIGHTEOUSNESS.
                                    —JEREMIAH 23:6

For He made Him who knew no sin to be sin
for us, that we might become the righteousness of God in Him.
                              —2 CORINTHIANS 5:21

The word *righteous* has gotten a bad rap over the years.
Too many now believe it is defined by a list of things
we are against rather than a state of being. It has been
hijacked by the "doers and don'ters" of the world and
turned into justification of hatred for the marginal-
ized or even the wealthy. It has become the property of
politics, hidden below the surface, but epitomized in
every speech, book, or broadcast about how our side is
"right" and the other side is not. This "right-eous-ness" is
used time and again to divide, manipulate, and exploit.
We become cogs in another piece of machinery where
someone else is pushing the buttons.

However, the true power of the word *righteous* is not in relationship to facts, truths, or platforms, but it is in relationship to other people and to God. Its foundational precept is in being right with God—the quality of being in right relationship with Him is *righteousness*. The problem we face is that it is easier to be in line with—or "right" with—a static principle than it is to be right with a living God. Principles of right and wrong are like light switches—they are either on or off; things are either good or bad. While sin is bad and corrupts the individual, a good God has the power to look at what is in the person's life and offer to forgive it and bring the person back into "right standing"—back into relationship. It is the extension of the scepter by the highest judge in the land to the person who enters the throne room without permission. It isn't that He is blind to the offense, but in the face of the offense He chooses to grant pardon because the debt of the offense has already been paid.

There is no better example of "The Lord Our Righteousness"—*Jehovah Tsidkenu* in the Hebrew language—than Jesus Christ, who took our sin upon Himself "that we might become the righteousness of God in Him" (2 Cor. 5:21). The curtain that divided the holy of holies was ripped from top to bottom to show that we were no longer separated from the presence of God. Jesus's sacrifice on the cross threw open the throne room of God to any who would enter. Relationship with our Father was restored. But our righteousness is not based upon our own deeds, behavior, or believing the right things—it is based on what Jesus did. Only in Him are we righteous and able to enter the court of heaven to plead our case before the ultimate King and judge. Thus God *is* our righteousness; He Himself is the reason we can approach the throne, and He is the ultimate right answer to whatever question is being asked.

THE LORD IS PRESENT

All the way around shall be eighteen thousand cubits; and the name of the city from that day shall be: THE LORD IS THERE.
—EZEKIEL 48:35

Let your conduct be without covetousness; be content with such things as you have. For He Himself has said, "I will never leave you nor forsake you." So we may boldly say: "The

Lord is my helper; I will not fear. What can man do to me?"

—Hebrews 13:5-6

The name *Jehovah Shammah* speaks not just of God's omnipresence but also His proximity to every question at hand. The above passage in Ezekiel speaks of a future city that would be named "The Lord Is There" to represent that the presence of God would always be in that city. However, centuries later Augustine took the term "City of God" to represent not a place but a people. He contrasted the "City of God" upon the earth with the "City of Man" to express the ways of God versus the ways of the world. Thus it was the people who welcomed and embraced the presence of God versus those who rejected it and wanted to go their own way.

While in God's presence there is healing, freedom, and wholeness, too often we forget it is also a place of conviction, heartbreak, and refining. Just as an athlete "feels the burn" that cuts away the fat and builds muscle, so being in the presence of God burns away the cancer of sin to build our spiritual aptitudes and abilities. Going into that place of intercession is similar to going to the gym for our human spirits. There is a place where you "feel the burn" and it feels good, but at the same time you know there are "unwanted pounds" that are being burned away in the process. In the process we:

> ...lay aside every weight, and the sin which so easily ensnares us, and...run with endurance the race that is set before us, looking unto Jesus, the author and finisher of our faith, who for the joy that was set before Him endured the cross, despising the shame, and has sat down at the right hand of the throne of God.
>
> —HEBREWS 12:1–2

If we would but develop a sense of the presence of God with us at all times, wherever we go, we would in fact become radical agents of God's change. Certainly most of us know what it is like to be in church and feel the presence of God, but what about in our workplaces, in our homes, or walking through our communities? God is no less there than He is at church. Perhaps it is not what God is doing that needs to change, but what we are doing. This is certainly one area where we have to take God at His name.

IN HIS NAME

So why does God give us all these different names? *Because it is His intent to be all of these things to you and me*—provision, presence, power, might, healing, guidance, right-standing, peace, help, sanctification, and victory. And He is the judge who presides over the court of heaven. When we approach Him, God wants us to see Him for who He is—understand His identity—and not focus on our own shortcomings or needs. It enables us to take our eyes off the problem and fix them instead on the solution. Do you or someone you know need financial help or guidance? Seek *Jehovah Jireh*. Do you or someone you know need healing? Seek *Jehovah Rophe*. Do you know someone who needs a victory in their lives? Seek *Jehovah Nissi*. After all, it is God we need to get ahold of, not just what He can provide.

I believe this is why Jesus told us to pray in His name—because His name carries the authority of His Father, and, as He put it, "He who has seen Me has seen the Father" (John 14:9). It is through Jesus we are given the right to approach God, for He is the one who made us right with God. He wants us to be

His fruitful representatives on the earth. As He told
His disciples:

> I chose you and appointed you that you
> should go and bear fruit, and that your fruit
> should remain, that whatever you ask the
> Father in My name He may give you.
> —JOHN 15:16

If anything, get rid of any idea that God is a can-
tankerous old man sitting on His throne looking
for people to punish. God simply isn't that kind of
a judge. He is looking for people to vindicate. He is
looking for people in whom He can show Himself
strong. Faith is based at least partially on knowing
"He is a rewarder of those who diligently seek Him"
(Heb. 11:6). And let me tell you, that is exactly who
intercessors are: diligent seekers of God.

So, now that you know who He is, how should
you, as Esther did, prepare yourself to enter into His
throne room?

THREE

DRESSED FOR SUCCESS

Clothed in Righteousness

*I will greatly rejoice in the LORD, my soul
shall be joyful in my God; for He has clothed
me with the garments of salvation, He has
covered me with the robe of righteousness, as a
bridegroom decks himself with ornaments, and
as a bride adorns herself with her jewels.*

ISAIAH 61:10

*The Holy Ghost does not flow through
methods, but through men. He does not come
on machinery, but on men. He does not
anoint plans, but men—men of prayer.*[1]

E. M. BOUNDS

One plus God equals a majority.

AUTHOR UNKNOWN

THERE IS SOMETHING to making a formal entrance. When Esther dressed to come before King Ahasuerus, she wasn't just dressing up for a romantic dinner at home, as unusual as that might be. No, she was preparing herself as an ambassador about to speak to a king on behalf of her people. In preparation, she didn't just pick out her best gown and make sure her makeup was right. She fasted and prayed three days before she went in. She came in with a plan of action. She was willing to lavish so much time on the king that he would ask her what her petition was rather than having to present it herself. She was not going to be denied. Every wile she had would be employed in seeing that her petition was granted.

It is not hard to see that this is very different from how most of us approach prayer today. There is no question that God wants us to come to Him daily, just as we are, but there is also something to be said for coming to prayer with a long-range plan and entering like a diplomatic ambassador or an attorney representing a client. Those who have the most successful and fulfilling prayer lives are not those who pray only when some problem comes up. For them, to be alive is to pray. The great reformer Martin

Luther said it this way, "To be a Christian without prayer is no more possible than to be alive without breathing."[2] Andrew Murray wrote, "Prayer is the pulse of life; by it the doctor can tell what is the condition of the heart."[3] Prayer is not something we add onto our Christianity; it and Scripture are the primary roots by which our Christianity is real. How can we hope to do the will of heaven if we are never in communication with it? How are we to obey God if we cannot decipher what He is speaking to us?

Intercession is the dogged, persistent type of prayer that comes before the Father time and again until an assurance of the answer is won in the spirit. It is a formal petition that has an official bearing. It can be a continued assault—praying and fasting through the night—or it can be a siege of heaven that happens day after day, week after week, year after year until God Himself impresses on you that the matter is taken care of, whether it has manifested itself in the natural yet or not.

According to prayer warrior Rees Howells, intercession is made up of three things: (1) an intense identification with those you are interceding for, (2) the agony of staying in prayer until the battle is won and release comes into the intercessor's spirit, and

(3) the authority that is won when the "intercession is gained."[4] The highest example of this identification comes in how Jesus came to earth as a human being. He was born a vulnerable, fragile infant and went on to pay for humanity's sin with every blow and every stripe of the lash He took from the Roman soldiers, only then to face agony of the cross. At any time He could have called legions of angels to rescue Him, but He did not. There was a greater purpose to His incarnation. He stayed human to the very end—stayed in intercession—and suffered every wound in our place until "it was finished."

Moses did the same thing when he prayed, offering himself in the place of the people of Israel, standing between them and the judgment they deserved:

> Then Moses returned to the LORD and said, "Oh, these people have committed a great sin, and have made for themselves a god of gold! Yet now, if You will forgive their sin—but if not, I pray, blot me out of Your book which You have written."
> —EXODUS 32:31–32

Now that Jesus has paid for sin, our intercession is in the spirit and to agree with the cross that the debt has already been paid for in full. We have but to stand until the light of Christ breaks through in any given situation.

The Jesus of the cross—the Jesus who took sin on headfirst—is not the same picture of Jesus that we get when He tells the disciples to let the little children come to Him: "Let the little children come to me and do not hinder them, for to such belongs the kingdom of heaven" (Matt. 19:14, ESV). No, instead, this is a Jesus dreadful to evil and fully understanding the corrupting power of sin. Oswald Chambers described this uncomfortable, uncompromising Christ in this way:

> There is an aspect of Jesus that chills the heart of a disciple to the core and makes the whole spiritual life gasp for breath. This strange Being with His face set like a flint and His striding determination strikes terror into me. He is no longer Counselor and Comrade, He is taken up with a point of view I know nothing about, and I am amazed at Him. At first I was confident that I understood Him, but now I am not so sure. I begin to realize there is a distance between Jesus Christ and me; I can no longer be familiar with Him. He

is ahead of me and He never turns round; I have no idea where He is going, and the goal has become strangely far off.

Jesus Christ had to fathom every sin and every sorrow man could experience, and that is what makes Him seem strange. When we see Him in this aspect we do not know Him, we do not recognize one feature of his life, and we do not know how to begin to follow Him. He is on in front, a Leader who is very strange, and we have no comradeship with Him.[5]

This does not mean our friendship with Christ in nullified, only that we do not recognize this dreadful Savior in our normal, everyday Christianity. This is a Jesus very different from the one we usually hear about in church. This is the Christ who is jealous for the people of the earth, the One who sits night and day beside the Father in heaven and intercedes for the earth. This is the Christ we emulate in prayer—our faces set like flint to stand for others, fear inspiring in our intensity, relentless on the powers of darkness. D. L. Moody said it this way, "Prayer means that I am to be raised up into feeling, into union and design with Him; that I am to enter into His counsel, and carry out His purpose fully."[6]

THE ARMOR OF PRAYER

In the last chapter of Ephesians Paul instructs that we need to enter into prayer for others as if going to battle. We are to be dressed in the armor of our faith. He tells us:

> Finally, my brethren, be strong in the Lord and in the power of His might. Put on the whole armor of God, that you may be able to stand against the wiles of the devil.... Therefore take up the whole armor of God, that you may be able to withstand in the evil day, and having done all, to stand.
>
> —EPHESIANS 6:10–11, 13

Then he goes on to describe each of the different components of that armor:

> Stand therefore, having girded your waist with truth, having put on the breastplate of righteousness, and having shod your feet with the preparation of the gospel of peace; above all, taking the shield of faith with which you will be able to quench all the fiery darts of the wicked one. And take the helmet of salvation, and the sword of the Spirit, which is the word

63

of God; praying always with all prayer and supplication in the Spirit, being watchful to this end with all perseverance and supplication for all the saints.

—EPHESIANS 6:14–18

When we come to prayer, truth is what we are wrapped in and what holds the pieces of our armor in place. The truth that we are right with God through the atoning sacrifice of Jesus Christ is what protects our hearts from doubt and indecisiveness. Everywhere we walk, we are to remember that our purpose is the *shalom* peace that God chose as His own name. Faith is what protects us from the counterattacks of the enemy and behind which we charge forward in the face of fear. The sword we wield is the promises of the Word of God, for they are the laws and precepts of the kingdom of heaven by which we tell the court of heaven we have a right to receive whatever we are asking. Clad like this, we are ready to face any battlefront and call down the light of heaven to make change. And, as we wrap ourselves in these things, we start to become just who God put us on the earth to be: His representatives on the earth, reflections in word and deed of

His Son. In this passage in Ephesians Paul even uses language from the Book of Isaiah that was spoken about the coming Messiah, Jesus:

> Then the LORD saw it, and it displeased Him
> That there was no justice.
> He saw that there was no man,
> And wondered that there was no intercessor;
> Therefore His own arm brought salvation for
>   Him;
> And His own righteousness, it sustained
>   Him.
> For He put on righteousness as a breastplate,
> And a helmet of salvation on His head;
> He put on the garments of vengeance for
>   clothing,
> And was clad with zeal as a cloak....
> "The Redeemer will come to Zion,
> And to those who turn from transgression in
>   Jacob,"
> Says the LORD.
>
> —ISAIAH 59:15–17, 20

As a rule, we grossly underestimate the power of our prayers for others. God calls us into the dance and dialogue of intercession, because He is looking for partners on the earth to reach out and save those

He loves on the earth, standing between them and catastrophe. He wants sons and daughters on the earth after the likeness of the incarnate Christ. Jesus, after all, "always lives to make intercession" (Heb. 7:25). If we strive to be like Him, shouldn't we also be interceding? When we truly "put on Christ" (Gal. 3:27), we must also put on intercession, because that is what He does day and night. It is, after all, the foundational power for bringing change out of the spirit into our physical world. It is the work of every believer. It is the key to the expansion of the kingdom of God. And it is the foundation of a life worth living.

Not only that, but you can't make such petitions of heaven without resolve and without it changing you. In his book *With Christ in the School of Prayer* Andrew Murray called intercessory prayer "faith's training-school." He goes on to say:

> There our friendship with men and with God is tested. There it is seen whether my friendship with the needy is so real, that I will take time and sacrifice my rest, will go even at midnight and not cease until I have obtained for them what I need. There it is seen whether my friendship with God is so clear, that I

can depend on Him not to turn me away and therefore pray on until He gives.

O what a deep heavenly mystery this is of persevering prayer. The God who has promised, who longs, whose fixed purpose it is to give the blessing, holds it back. It is to Him a matter of such deep importance that His friends on earth should know and fully trust their rich Friend in heaven, that He trains them, in the school of answer delayed, to find out how their perseverance really does prevail, and what the mighty power is they can wield in heaven, if they do but set themselves to it. There is a faith that sees the promise, and embraces it, and yet does not receive it (Heb. xi.13, 39). It is when the answer to prayer does not come, and the promise we are most firmly trusting appears to be of none effect, that the trial of faith, more precious than of gold, takes place. It is in this trial that the faith that has embraced the promise is purified and strengthened and prepared in personal, holy fellowship with the living God, to see the glory of God. It takes and holds the promise until it has received the fulfillment of

what it had claimed in a living truth in the
unseen but living God.[7]

This is no trivial matter. Even if we come to intercession the same second we hear of the need of
another, we must put on the mind-set of faith that
says our words will do more than just send vibrations into the air. We must recognize that we have
a place before the throne of God and a right to be
there. We must recognize there are promises of God
that apply—spiritual laws that can be relied upon to
bring help in the time of need. And you must, just as
Esther did, come with the resolve that you will not
be denied—after all, you have God's Word on it.

Four

"WHAT'S NEXT, PAPA?"

The Adventure of Prayer in the Spirit

God's Spirit beckons. There are things to do and places to go! This resurrection life you received from God is not a timid, grave-tending life. It's adventurously expectant, greeting God with a childlike "What's next, Papa?" God's Spirit touches our spirits and confirms who we really are.

ROMANS 8:14–16, THE MESSAGE

God can work wonders if he can get a suitable man. Men can work wonders if they can get God to lead them. The full endowment of the spirit that turned the world upside down would be eminently useful in these latter days. Men who can stir things mightily for God, whose spiritual revolutions change the whole aspect of things, are the universal need of the church.[1]

E. M. BOUNDS

IN THE THIRD and fourth chapters of the Book of Galatians Paul talks about what it means to grow up in Christ, going from a child tutored by the dos and don'ts of the Scriptures toward an adult who lives in grace by faith as God's own cherished son or daughter. We were in guardianship of the Law as we grew up, but as we became adults, we found we could relate to God for ourselves, not tossing the laws of God aside but instead being able to go straight to their source in the presence of our Father. When a child is young, right and wrong are very black and white; at that stage of life it is really all our minds can comprehend. A thing either is or it isn't; the light is either on or it's off. But as we grow up, our minds become open to nuances, and an understanding of the Law deepens our perspectives. It is not that the Law changes, but we begin to understand the purpose of the Law and the spirit behind it. We can place it in relationship with other laws and derive from them a sense of living by them that goes beyond what they literally tell us to do or what they each mean on their own. Instead of living by a legal code of fulfilling the "letter" of the Law, we begin to plug into the "spirit" of what God is saying to us through His Word. As Paul put it:

> The law was our guardian until Christ came,
> in order that we might be justified by faith.
> But now that faith has come, we are no longer
> under a guardian, for in Christ Jesus you are
> all sons of God, through faith.
>
> —GALATIANS 3:24–26, ESV

Sons and daughters differ from orphans in that they know their parents and can relate to them. Faith in what Jesus did—that He atoned for our sin and gave us "right standing" with God once again so that we could be in His presence and converse with Him through prayer—puts us in connection with our Father. Grace covers the deficit between whatever bad mistakes we have made in the past and our relationship with God. This is the place of true freedom. Or as Paul goes on to say:

> The heir, as long as he is a child, is no different from a slave, though he is the owner of everything, but he is under guardians and managers until the date set by his father. In the same way we also, when we were children [immature], were enslaved to the elementary principles of the world. But when the fullness of time had come, God sent forth his Son…to

redeem those who were under the law, so that we might receive adoption as sons. And because you are sons, God has sent the Spirit of his Son into our hearts, crying, "Abba! Father!" So you are no longer a slave, but a son, and if a son, then an heir through God.

—GALATIANS 4:1–7, ESV

When we are immature, we look at Scripture as a book of dos and don'ts, and we live by a "code" of Christianity. It is a religion, in that it is our own understanding of what to do to pursue God and how to act in order to please Him. Religion is thus humanity, in our own wisdom, reaching out toward God the best that we can. In and of itself this is not always a bad thing—it is one way sincere people pursue God as best they can—but if we never allow God to breathe into our religion His way of reaching out toward humanity, it is often more of a stumbling block than a help. For years John Wesley fumbled after God in just this way, creating his own "methods" for pursuing God as he understood from church tradition and the Bible, but then one day while attending a Moravian society meeting, where they were reading from Martin Luther's preface to the

Book of Romans, the revelation of God's method of reaching out to humanity touched his heart, and as he described it, he felt his "heart strangely warmed." As he expounded upon this feeling, "I felt I did trust in Christ, Christ alone, for salvation; and an assurance was given me that He had taken away my sins, even mine, and saved me from the law of sin and death."[2] Until that point John had lived under the guardianship of his disciplines in seeking God, but his lack of genuine connection was a continual stumbling block. However, when his disciplined habits were breathed on by God, things changed quickly. Within a matter of a few years—months really— John was at the center of one of the greatest times of societal change the world has ever experienced: the Great Awakening.

I also really like how Eugene Peterson paraphrases the last couple of verses of this passage:

> You can tell for sure that you are now fully adopted as his own children because God sent the Spirit of his Son into our lives crying out, "Papa! Father!" Doesn't that privilege of intimate conversation with God make it plain that you are not a slave, but a child? And if

you are a child, you're also an heir, with complete access to the inheritance.

—Galatians 4:6–7, The Message

Maturing from a simple seeker of God and follower of His directives, we become children in relationship to Him who have the "privilege of intimate conversation with God" through prayer. We can go to Him and say, "Dad, I have a question," or "Dad, can you help me with this for a minute?" Being right with Him allows us to converse with Him about the most private or complex of issues. Can we really afford to lay that privilege aside and not regularly enter His throne room with whatever concern we might have? Should we neglect our access to heaven and the authority and privileges that go with that for the distractions of this world? This is the responsibility of intercession, but it is also just the first glimpse of the real adventure of it.

The Three Works of Grace

Grace is one of the most powerful concepts in the Bible, and while many of us have a very good understanding of the first work of grace, not enough of us understand its other two. Many of us practice them without realizing it, but I think to understand all of grace is to understand intercession. It is also to be catapulting into the type of life God really wants for us—a life of transformation, power, and abundance.

The first work of grace is what we receive when we come to Christ in the first place. It is powerful beyond measure. It delivers us from whatever mess we have gotten ourselves into that has forced alienation from God and back into right standing with Him. It is this work of grace that overcomes all of the sin in our lives and opens the lines between us and heaven once again. It delivers the sinner to the foot of the cross by nothing more than that we accepted Jesus as our Lord and Savior, giving our lives to Him. It is grace that saves us from ourselves and our bad decisions. As Paul put it:

> For by grace you have been saved through faith, and that not of yourselves; it is the gift of God, not of works, lest anyone should boast.
>
> —EPHESIANS 2:8–9

It is this work of grace that delivers us through the gate of the kingdom of God into His realm. We have crossed the threshold from darkness into light. We have signed our names to the writ of adoption He freely offers to become His child.

This first work of grace is marvelous and powerful, but too few realize that this deliverance from darkness and separation from God is not all grace has to offer us. Too many Christians live in a cycle of this grace alone, stumbling back and forth between sin and salvation, darkness and light, separation from God and reuniting with Him. I don't mean losing your salvation and getting it back again—what I am saying is that we have this tendency to fall out of communion with God because of our choices, and then return to Him, rededicate our lives to Him, and return to relating with Him once again. However, then, because we know little else, we then stumble back into sin again, feel separated from Him and powerless, until the next time we feel the emotional surge of His love and presence to then give ourselves to Him one more time. It is a cycle the devil loves— Christian who are "saved" in an eternal sense but who do very little damage to his kingdom on the earth. Soldiers with powerful weapons but no ammunition. A people with big dreams, but no plan of action to accomplish them. A people who are righteous in the eyes of heaven but who fail to exercise heaven's authority upon the earth.

But if we look at the next verse in this passage on grace in Ephesians, we see the next work of grace:

> For we are His workmanship, created in Christ Jesus for good works, which God prepared beforehand that we should walk in them.
> —EPHESIANS 2:10

You see, the second work of grace is the ability to become who God designed us to be. *Vine's Expository Dictionary* adds this definition of *grace* to the saving grace that delivers us from sin back into relationship with God. According to it, *grace* is also:

> …the spiritual state of those who have experienced its exercise, whether (1) a state of "grace,"…or (2) a proof thereof in practical effects, deeds of "grace,"…(the sum of earthly blessings); the power and equipment for ministry.[3]

When it says ministry here, it is not just talking about pastors, missionaries, and those who work full-time for a church or "ministry"; it means anything that is the work of manifesting the kingdom of heaven on the earth. It is the second work of grace that enables every Christian to do God's will. In the New Living Translation the "workmanship" in Ephesians 2:10 is instead translated "masterpiece." I think that says a lot.

> We are God's masterpiece. He has created us anew in Christ Jesus, so we can do the good things he planned for us long ago.
> —Ephesians 2:10, nlt

This talks about us as a "masterpiece" created by God to perform a great work He had planned for us to accomplish from the beginning of time.

The Book of Romans is full of references to this. Look at this example:

> God decided on this course of action in full view of the public—to set the world in the clear with himself through the sacrifice of Jesus, finally taking care of the sins he had so patiently endured. This is not only clear, but it's now—this is current history! God sets

things right. He also makes it possible for us
to live in his rightness.
—ROMANS 3:25–26, THE MESSAGE

Both of the first two works are illustrated in this
passage:

1. God sets things right.

2. He makes it possible for us to live in
   His rightness.

I believe the difference between the form of
Christianity that stumbles back and forth between
the ways of this world and regaining fellowship with
God and the form of Christianity that is actively
working His good upon the earth is a consistent,
disciplined prayer life. How are we to do God's will
without downloading His plans and strategies from
heaven on a regular basis? How are we to be His representatives on the earth without daily building His
characteristics into our lives in the "workout room"
of the Holy Spirit? We must have His wisdom, attri-
butes, and knowledge of His specific will for any situation if we are to see His plans walked out in the
world around us.

Charles Finney talked about this function of prayer as a means into the mind of Christ:

> The more we pray, the more shall we be enlightened, for surely they are most enlightened who pray most. If we go no farther in divine things than human reason can carry us, we get little indeed from God.
>
> The more men pray, the more they will love prayer, and the more will they enjoy God. On the other hand, the more we pray—in real prayer—the more will God delight in us.
>
> Observe this which I say: Delight; the more will God truly DELIGHT in us.
>
> This is not merely the love of benevolence, for God is benevolent to all; but He delights in His praying children in the sense of having complacency in their character. The Bible often speaks of the great interest which God takes in those who live near Him in much prayer. This is naturally and necessarily the case. Why should not God delight in those who delight in Him?
>
> The more we pray, the more God loves to manifest to others that He delights in us, and hears our prayers. If His children live lives of much prayer, God delights to honour them,

as an encouragement to others to pray. They come into a position in which He can bless them and can make His blessings on them result in good to others—thus doubly gratifying the benevolence of His heart.[4]

So, if you were thinking of this on a continuum, the first act of prayer takes you from where you were in sin before knowing God back into relationship—or "right standing"—with Him. The second work of grace is for the person back in relationship with Him to commune with Him in prayer, get His plans and strategies for his or her life, and walk them out on the earth. This means going from the place of reuniting with Him through salvation toward fulfilling His purpose for your life. This second work is the path of holiness before God. We become the person God always intended us to be: *perfect*—think "mature, grown up"—in His sight, walking out His will, expanding His kingdom.

So what is the third work of grace? That is the grace of God we extend to others. For some, that means we offer them the grace that first saved us. For others, that means helping them from the gateway of the kingdom of God toward the heart of it—helping them realize their purposes and walk in them. It also means we live a life of grace, constantly extending grace, just as Jesus did when He walked the earth. We are not easily offended—which is one of Satan's most powerful stumbling blocks—we easily go the extra mile when we feel led to, and we live in the *shalom* peace of partnership with God and others. We don't get preoccupied with titles or positions, we honor all people as works in progress along the way toward becoming "God's masterpieces," and we are living, breathing gospel letters to the people around us, written by God's own hand. This is the life of an intercessor who not only practices these things in a "prayer closet" but also walks them out continually throughout the day, effectively "praying without ceasing." As John Wesley described this:

> God's command to pray without ceasing is founded on the necessity we have of his grace to preserve the life of God in the soul, which can no more subsist one moment without it, than the body can without air.
>
> Whether we think of, or speak to, God, whether we act or suffer for him, all is prayer, when we have no other object than his love, and the desire of pleasing him.

All that a Christian does, even in eating and sleeping, is prayer, when it is done in simplicity, according to the order of God, without either adding to or diminishing from it by his own choice.

Prayer continues in the desire of the heart, though the understanding be employed on outward things.

In souls filled with love, the desire to please God is a continual prayer.

As the furious hate which the Devil bears us is termed the roaring of a lion, so our vehement love may be termed, crying after God.[5]

Thus I believe the highest form of living for God is birthed in intercession, praying constantly for the things God has put on our hearts for ourselves and others, but also with an ever expectant openness to God that says constantly, "What's next, Papa?" It is the God-life as Jesus Himself described it:

Embrace this God-life. Really embrace it, and nothing will be too much for you. This mountain, for instance: Just say, "Go jump in the lake"—no shuffling or shilly-shallying—and it's as good as done. That's why I urge you to pray for absolutely everything, ranging from small to large. Include everything as you embrace this God-life, and you'll get God's everything.

—MARK 11:22–24, THE MESSAGE

I believe this sets the stage for our entering into the presence of God to intercede just as Esther did before her king and husband. Now that we better understand how to enter in, what will be our plan of attack once we get there?

PART TWO

THE DISCIPLINE OF INTERCESSION

Prayer has failed. We are on slippery ground. Only intercession will avail. God is calling for intercessors—men and women who will lay their lives on the altar to fight the devil, as really as they would have to fight on the Western Front.[1]

—REES HOWELLS,

in an address to the student body
on March 29, 1936, as Hitler began
to flex his military power

FIVE

FIRST OF ALL

Those in Authority

*The first thing I want you to do is pray. Pray every
way you know how, for everyone you know. Pray
especially for rulers and their governments to
rule well so we can be quietly about our business
of living simply, in humble contemplation. This
is the way our Savior God wants us to live.*

1 TIMOTHY 2:1–3,
THE MESSAGE

*Scripture calls us to pray for many things: for all
saints; for all men; for kings and all rulers; for
all who are in adversity; for the sending forth
of labourers; for those who labour in the gospel;
for all converts; for believers who have fallen
into sin; for one another in our own immediate
circles. The Church is now so much larger than
when the New Testament was written; the
number of forms of work and workers is so much
greater; the needs of the Church and the world*

are so much better known, that we need to take
time and thought to see where prayer is needed,
and to what our heart is most drawn out.[1]

ANDREW MURRAY

THERE IS NO question that entering into deep intercession does not happen without a disciplined prayer life. Praying without ceasing does not completely cover this. While there will be times we will enter intercession on a spur-of-the-moment prompting, most intercession will take place in times of regular, premeditated, habitual prayer.

With prayer such an important part of our faith, it is somewhat surprising how little actual instruction we get on prayer in the Scriptures. I think a big part of this is that the school of prayer is prayer itself. As Charles Spurgeon once said, "Pray until you can really pray." It is something you learn to do by doing more than by being instructed in doing. You learn to walk the "way" or "path" of prayer as I discussed in the second chapter of my book *The Art of*

War for Spiritual Battle. While I still believe instruction on prayer can be very valuable—or else, of course, I wouldn't write books on the topic—I think the instruction makes little sense until you have a regular, dedicated time of prayer you practice in your daily life.

At the same time, the Scriptures do have some rather important things to say about the practice of prayer. In the Gospels Jesus gives us the Lord's Prayer—which is what we call it, but in fact, it is really the "disciple's prayer" as He gives it to us for our prayer lives, not for His.[2] While repeating that prayer from memory is good, I think it is even better to use it as an outline for Holy Spirit–led prayer. In that light we enter prayer with praise and worship, "hallowing" the name of the Father. Or as the psalmist described it:

> Enter into His gates with thanksgiving,
> And into His courts with praise.
> —Psalm 100:4

The second part of that prayer tells us to pray:

> Your kingdom come.
> Your will be done
> On earth as it is in heaven.
> —Matthew 6:10

I believe it is this part of our regular prayer times that Paul discusses and explains in 1 Timothy:

> This charge I commit to you, son Timothy, according to the prophecies previously made concerning you, that by them you may wage the good warfare, having faith and a good conscience....
>
> Therefore I exhort first of all that supplications, prayers, intercessions, and giving of thanks be made for all men, for kings and all who are in authority, that we may lead a quiet and peaceable life in all godliness and reverence. For this is good and acceptable in the sight of God our Savior, who desires all men to be saved and to come to the knowledge of the truth.
>
> —1 Timothy 1:18–19; 2:1–4

I find it quite interesting that Paul and Jesus agree that our first priority in prayer is not to go through our prayer list of personal sins, needs, and concerns, but to first take a global perspective of praying for governments, economies, and our societies, or more specifically, the people who impact them the most. We are instructed to pray for presidents, kings, and other leaders, "that we may lead a quiet and peaceable life in all godliness and reverence." When our leadership is right, the hindrances to the manifestation of the kingdom of God on the earth are greatly reduced. Great things happen when we live in a godly society governed by godly leaders.

In the United States we have fallen into the trap of thinking that our power to vote is greater than our power in prayer. Too many save their season of prayer for election season, praying that we will get the right people or party into office; then we judge the success or failure of our prayers based on whether our candidates won or not. If they did, we celebrate; if they didn't, we think our prayers failed. However, did you know there were Christians in the other party who were praying for their candidates in the same way? Our opinion is often that they were simply wrong or misunderstood the true issues, but I think we are all missing the point if we feel that way. While praying at election times is a good thing, we are making a big mistake if that is the only time we are praying for our government. The truth is, we should actually be praying more *between* elections than we pray for them.

Note that Paul doesn't tell us here to pray that the right people come into leadership. The reason for this is, no matter who is elected, regardless of their character, their political principles, or their religious beliefs, they are going to face challenging decisions, vying influences from diverse, conflicting factions, and temptations greater than normal citizens will every face. As Spider-Man says, "With great power comes great responsibility."[3] On the other hand, as Lord John Acton put it, "Power tends to corrupt, and absolute power corrupts absolutely. Great men are almost always bad men."[4] Whether we elect "good" people or not, whether we elect the "right" people or not, they are going to face corrupting influences. They don't need our prayers as much to get them elected as they do to keep them—or get them onto— the right paths that will allow all in their governance to "lead a quiet and peaceable life in all godliness and reverence." This is so important, God even told us Himself:

> If My people who are called by My name will humble themselves, and pray and seek My face, and turn from their wicked ways, then I will hear from heaven, and will forgive their sin and heal their land.
>
> —2 Chronicles 7:14

Because of this, God puts prayer for our government leaders at the top of our prayer lists, then for our spiritual leaders, and only then for our families, friends, and loved ones. This overarching approach also helps us love others first as well, making praying for the common good a priority after seeking God.

PRESIDENTS, KINGS, AND ALL WHO ARE IN AUTHORITY

For this reason I have found it a good idea to keep a prayer list with me at all times that is both easy to access and easy to update. This may be a sheet you have typed up and printed off of your computer and slipped into your Bible or prayer journal, a file on your smartphone or tablet, a page in your planner, or some other method that works with however you organize yourself. (This is also a great place to record scriptures you are standing on or that God has given you to pray for others.) Then do a little research on the Internet and find the names of the following people and their spouses:

- Your president, prime minister, or top-ranking official

- ◆ Members of their cabinet, ministries, or advisors

- ◆ Your vice president

- ◆ Heads of your congressional branches or parliamentary houses

- ◆ Congressmen, senators, or MPs from your state, province, district, or county

- ◆ The governor or head of your state, province, or territory

- ◆ The representatives for your area to your state or local congressional assembly

- ◆ Your county commissioners or leadership

- ◆ The mayor of your city, town, or village

Once you have this, start to think of pastors and churches in your area and add them to your list. Are their ministries or nonprofit organizations that you give to regularly (like Trimm International ☺)? Add them to your list, as well as the names of the leaders of those organizations. Put your own pastor and spouse at the top of that list. Then spend some time in prayer and ask God if there is anyone else you should have on that list.

Once you have this, pull it out whenever you have your regular time of prayer or in downtimes like riding the bus or subway, during your breaks at work, when you are standing in line, or other times like that. There will be times you simply read through this list to raise them up before the throne, but also be open to God leading you into specific times of prayer for each of these people.

Then, as you watch the news, read your newspaper, or check out the Internet sites that keep you up-to-date with what is happening in the world, watch for issues or concerns you can add to this list or that people on your prayer list are struggling with. I firmly believe that Christians have very little business watching or reading the news as anything other than something that will tie directly into what they are praying for (except, of course, for things like the weather or sports scores). There should be very little pain and suffering we experience on this earth that we don't at least lift up to God momentarily and say something along the lines of, "God, reach out to those people and help them through being present with them."

Scripture tells us:

> The king's heart is in the hand of the LORD,
> Like the rivers of water;
> He turns it wherever He wishes.
>
> —PROVERBS 21:1

And I believe that goes for anyone in a leadership position anywhere. Lift them up to God. Hold them before God and ask He make them accountable. Pray that God speaks to them and gives them wisdom. Find scriptures to write in by their names, and pray them every day. Or, if nothing else, sit and listen to the Spirit and ask Him what you should be praying for that person and their families. Oh, that we were people of such continual prayer! What a difference it would make for our nations, communities, and world!

A BURDEN TO PRAY OR A BURDEN OF GUILT?

Now, as I begin to address this issue of regular prayer, there is something else I need to discuss with you, and that is that attacks you will suffer because you have the courage to pray. There is nothing more dangerous to the kingdom of darkness then a praying church. Because of that, there is no tactic Satan won't use to keep you from praying. And not only that, when you are not praying, he will make you feel guilty for that! He wants to push you to one extreme or the other—anything to make your prayer life ineffective and burdensome or troublesome to you.

We need to remember that Jesus said:

> Come to Me, all you who labor and are heavy laden, and I will give you rest. Take My yoke upon you and learn from Me, for I am gentle and lowly in heart, and you will find rest for your souls. For My yoke is easy and My burden is light.
> —Matthew 11:28–30

When we go to God in prayer, there is a certain amount of squirming our earthly natures will do because prayer makes little sense to the natural mind and even less to our desires to be comfortable, engaged, and entertained. Even cleaning the kitchen or vacuuming looks better than spending time praying! It will take some discipline to get started and make it a regular part of your daily practice. And your calendar will fill up to try to push time for prayer out. Things will come up that need your "immediate attention" just as you get ready to spend some time in prayer. Don't let yourself get sidetracked. As Oswald Chambers cautioned:

> Beware of outstripping God by your very longing to do His will. We run ahead of Him in a thousand and one activities, consequently we get so burdened with persons and with difficulties that we do not worship God, we do not intercede. If once the burden and the pressure come upon us and we are not in the worshipping attitude, it will produce not only hardness toward God but despair in our own souls. God continually introduces us to people for whom we have no affinity, and unless we are worshipping God, the most natural thing to do is to treat them heartlessly, to give them a text like the jab of a spear, or leave them with a rapped-out counsel of God and go. A heartless Christian must be a terrible grief to Our Lord.[5]

At the same time, if you miss a prayer time, don't let guilt condemn you or discourage you. Don't feel like you have to spend all your day all the time in prayer or you are not pleasing God. If the devil can't keep you from praying, he will try to burn you out on it. He will try to make you feel so guilty that you become convinced you are a subpar Christian and don't have enough faith for God to answer your prayers.

Prayer may be a little difficult at first—as in the forming of any new habit you know will be good for you in the long run—but it should never be an overwhelming burden. In the history of prayer I am sure there have been one-word prayers more effective than hours of prayer at other times. If all you feel you have to pray is a few minutes, then pray those few minutes. Think about God throughout your day, and throw up little breath prayers. Start where you are, and grow in prayer. Pray with others. Go to prayer rooms or prayer meetings, and let the joy of being together with others lighten the resistance to prayer. But wherever you are, grow in prayer. Great men and women of prayer have always prayed, but each person's prayer journey is different. John "Praying" Hyde prayed through the night, night after night, and saw hundreds come to know Jesus, but Smith Wigglesworth, who operated powerfully in the gift of healing, was reported to have once scoffed at anyone who prayed more than twenty minutes at a time but then caught himself to comment, "But I doubt I ever go more than twenty minutes without praying!"

All that to say, don't let prayer become a burden to you. If you are faithful in it, there will be times God joins you in it and His presence will be so tangible you are afraid to move for fear it will leave. There is a joy in praying, and there is a joy in seeing your prayers answered. There is a comfort to others for you to spend time praying that they may never realize this side of heaven. Don't let things keep you from prayer, but at the same time don't let condemnation bury you in guilt that something about your prayers isn't really good enough. After all, for us as Christians, it is not about the time we spend in prayer or the fervency with which we pray; it is about the God to whom we pray. It is about connecting with Him and asking Him into our jurisdictions to establish His kingdom. Never get sidetracked from that true aim, and every moment you spend in prayer will have its own unique value and change even the times you aren't praying. That is the grace God offers to us. Pray with that grace, both for yourself and for others.

> God is able to make all grace abound toward you, that you, always having all sufficiency in all things, may have an abundance for every good work.
> —2 Corinthians 9:8

Six

BROTHERS AND
SISTERS IN CHAINS

Tackling World Issues in Prayer

*Real religion, the kind that passes muster
before God the Father, is this: Reach out to the
homeless and loveless in their plight, and guard
against corruption from the godless world.*

James 1:27,
The Message

*What is the reason that many thousands of
Christian workers in the world have not a greater
influence? Nothing save this—the prayerlessness
of their service. In the midst of all their zeal in
the study and in the work of the Church, of all
their faithfulness in preaching and conversation
with the people, they lack that ceaseless prayer,
which has attached to it the sure promise of
the Spirit and the power from on high. It is*

nothing but the sin of prayerlessness which is the cause of the lack of a powerful spiritual life![1]

Andrew Murray

Y<small>OU DON'T HAVE</small> to look far in our world today to find heart-wrenching issues that need God's light. While I believe that a good portion of intercession is for those in our immediate communities and our own nations, the world today is wracked by injustice, persecution, and exploitation. With modern communication technology virtually turning the world into a neighborhood, it is hard not to be touched by the plight of those half a world away, especially if they are children.

Let me give you some examples so you can see what I mean.

Human Trafficking

The world crime syndicates that traffic drugs and guns have found a new boon in trafficking human beings—either into slavery or prostitution. While drugs or guns are usually sold only once, women or children trapped in prostitution can be sold several times a day. It is estimated that there are more slaves on earth today than in the history of the world, a number somewhere around 27 million. The majority of these are women and children sold for sexual services, most under the age of eighteen.[2]

Right now this crime against humanity is perpetrated on every continent on the earth. If you live in a big city, chances are there is sex trafficking in your area, but it is equally prevalent at rural truck stops or in suburban homes neatly tucked away in nice neighborhoods. From time to time you will hear of restaurants that have been shut done because their entire labor force was imported from the Far East and worked as slaves in the kitchen.

Slavers prey particularly on the unattached. In Eastern Europe as changing economies forced parents to look for work in other countries, the new culture of "orphans" became ripe picking grounds for traffickers who cut deals with orphanage directors to kidnap young girls and import them into areas where prostitution is legal—showing that legalizing prostitution has the opposite effect of what is intended. Where sex is sold and regulated legally, illegal prostitution always thrives, especially the exploitation of children.[3]

In extremely poor areas such as Southeast Asia or South America it is not uncommon for a poor family to "sell" their children into prostitution in the larger cities in order to create a stream of income for themselves. In such areas girls and boys rescued from slavers and returned home often get sold back to slavers again.

The nation of Sweden recently took a revolutionary stance in labeling prostitution as a human rights violation—a crime against the dignity of women as a whole and individuals in particular, whether they chose to be prostitutes or not. In this light, they view sex workers as being exploited—so if a woman is arrested for prostitution, they offer rescue rather than punishment, while they have severe penalties for pimps and those looking to hire prostitutes. This has made Sweden and its neighboring nations rather unattractive to traffickers; while in areas such as Amsterdam and Bangkok the industry is still thriving.

This is an issue that needs revolutionary ideas, because in some areas it demands that core cultural values be addressed and transformed. If fathers and mothers can think it acceptable to sell their children, than something is wrong at a deep, fundamental level.

However, there is more and more attention being drawn to these issues, and organizations around the world are starting to address them in very real ways. Most of these organizations focus on three main areas: raising awareness, strategic intervention (by preventing kidnapping or recruitment), and restoration (by rescuing and rehabilitating victims). All of these efforts need our prayers and support.

One revolutionary idea I saw recently was the efforts of an abolitionist organization called Not For Sale who decided to address the temptation to sell children into slavery in the Amazon region. They felt that if they could create a viable, lasting source of income, many of the reasons for giving in to slavers would be eliminated. So, after a series of meetings with business leaders and other interested parties, the organization came up with the idea of creating a tea that could be harvested from the Amazon forests to sell in American health food stores and online called REBBL (which stands for "roots, extracts, berries, bark, and leaves"). You can find out more about it on the company's website at rebbltonic.com, or on Not For Sale's website at www.notforsale campaign.org.

One of the things I find remarkable about this endeavor is that in a very foundational way, Not For Sale isn't simply keeping children out of slavery but is addressing the culture of exploitation all together with a sustainable solution. Not only are they addressing the prevention, intervention, and restoration needed to stop the destruction of human trafficking, but they are also eliminating the need by empowering communities to pursue alternative economic opportunities. I like how one pastor from a persecuted nation put it: "I do not pray for a lighter load but for a stronger back." Just as Esther, rather than praying for rescue, made a request that would enable her people to save themselves, Not For Sale is doing that with their REBBL tea company.

Too often, when we want to help the needy, we think like charity organizations rather than innovators. I certainly never want to stop someone from giving to those in need, but we must also think about how to give a "hand up" rather than a "hand out." As the old saying goes, "Give a man a fish and he will eat for a day; teach him to fish and he will eat for a lifetime." As we approach issues like this, we should keep in mind the need to empower people to find a way out of their desperate situation themselves rather than simply providing a means of keeping them alive but trapped in the cycle of exploitation. Too seldom do we realize that God doesn't just intervene with His consoling presence or miracle-working power, but with ideas for alternative solutions and remarkable innovations that will transform cultures. While God will heal sickness and disease supernaturally, medicine and therapies to heal the sick or repair injuries also come from God's inspiration. You don't have to look far to find examples of extraordinary medical breakthroughs that came from devoted Christians looking to help and heal those who needed it most. As a rule, I have found human ideas can help for a moment, but God ideas can provide permanent solutions and empower people back to a place of self-determination and dignity.

Religious Persecution

The twentieth century saw more Christians die for their faith as gave their lives in all of Christian history combined.[4] A large reason for that was the rise of Communism and Socialism, which declared religion an "opiate of the people" and tried to "cleanse" their nations by purging them of Jews and Christians. This subsided somewhat in the latter half of the previous century, but as the twenty-first century has dawned, we are seeing the numbers rise again, mainly in the Arab world. The Arab Spring that happened not long ago hoped for democracy and more freedom, but the aftermath is thwarting those hopes, especially for Christians in those areas who are seeing rising persecution because extreme fundamentalist Islamic groups are gaining control. To be open about your Christianity now in such areas is to risk having your home set on fire or your family beaten. It is estimated that roughly 150,000 lose their lives each year as a result of being exposed as Christians.[5] That is more than 400 people every single day! Many times that number are harassed or imprisoned.

As I write this, a world plea is going up for a pastor imprisoned in Iran who is on death row for sharing his faith. A mother sits in prison in Pakistan—where she has been for over three years now—awaiting execution after being accused of blaspheming the prophet Muhammad because of her faith in Jesus. And these are just the stories that have caught the attention of the press. Others live in fear of police or mobs raiding their church gatherings or prayer meetings. Around the world courageous brothers and sisters know what it means to take up the cross and follow Jesus, for by so doing they risk their lives every day.

I urge you to check out the websites of organizations such as Open Doors or The Voice of the Martyrs and subscribe to their newsletters and prayer watch lists. Share the stories you find there with others, and encourage them to pray. Stand with these brothers and sisters in Christ to be strong in their faith and for God to guide them and lead them as they share His truth. Get involved with organizations fighting for the human right to practice the faith of their own convictions, for in such a free arena there is no doubt the gospel of Jesus Christ will prevail.

POVERTY AND HUNGER

Today in our world, despite the technology we have and the abundance of our planet, roughly 80 percent of people on earth live on less than ten dollars a day.[6] That is more than five billion people. On average, a child dies every four seconds from malnutrition or a preventable disease—roughly twenty-one thousand children each day.[7] That is not even counting those who die as bystanders in war zones or because of natural disasters, which always hit the poorest and most vulnerable the hardest. Over 780 million in the world don't have access to clean water,[8] and even more lack access to basic health care or a decent education.

Some look at poverty and say, "Well, Jesus told us the poor would always be with us." And that is true, but at the same time God also told Israel:

> There must be no poor people among you because GOD is going to bless you lavishly in this land that GOD, your God, is giving you as an inheritance, your very own land. But only if you listen obediently to the Voice of GOD, your God, diligently observing every commandment that I command you today.
> —DEUTERONOMY 15:4–5, THE MESSAGE

As part of a society that God has so richly blessed, it seems barbaric not to be disturbed there are children going to bed famished each night and others who won't wake up the next morning for reasons that are easily preventable.

At the same time, these numbers are dropping. In

the last twenty years extreme poverty has been cut in half.[9] In the World Health Organization (WHO) African Region death rates due to malaria have been reduced by 33 percent since the year 2000.[10] We have the medications, we have the technology, and change is happening. The trouble is, it is just not happening fast enough to save the children who will needlessly die today.

One of the biggest things in the way of keeping these numbers on a downward spiral is the global economic crisis we have faced in the last half decade. The money to keep these programs going is a small percentage of what it was a decade ago, and yet in the scramble for the United States to balance its national budget, this needed money is continually being cut (one more reason for us to pray for our leaders). Government corruption, mismanagement, and inefficiency challenge the implementation of the programs already in place. Corporate greed would rather funnel money into already overflowing coffers than allow it to flow to those who need it most. Are we going to simply float along getting swept up in the political finger-pointing that feeds the chaos, or are we willing to cut across party politics and be part of the solution our world needs? And, of course, it is not just about politics. There are other organizations doing good who need our financial support and prayers.

If current trends continue, we could see an end of extreme poverty before 2030—that means sometime in our lifetimes. But to keep this change on a positive track, we must be involved and voice our support in the hallways of both earthly and celestial governments.

Shalom in the Holy Land

Scripture plainly tells us:

> Pray for the peace of Jerusalem:
> "May they prosper who love you."
>
> —Psalm 122:6

And God told Abraham:

> I will bless those who bless you,
> And I will curse him who curses you;
> And in you all the families of the earth shall
> be blessed.
>
> —Genesis 12:3

Because of this, there is no question that praying for peace in Israel is something we all need to add to our intercessory prayer list. Since Israel became a nation again in 1948—a rather significant prophetic event in and of itself—there has been unrest between the Jews and the Arabs in the region over having a nation to call their own. Control of Jerusalem has been at the center of this struggle since the Israelis took back full ownership of it in 1967. From recent events as well, it doesn't look as if things will settle down or there will be a peaceful solution to the problems between the Arabs and the Jews any time soon. Regardless, we need to keep Jerusalem, Israel, and the Palestinians continually in our prayers and at the top of our prayer list of the nations we pray for regularly.

WHERE SHOULD WE FOCUS?

And, of course, there are many other issues just as important—just as threatening to life and freedom— some even in our own homes. Issues of domestic violence, drug abuse, incest, murder, rape, and other crimes—orphans created by war and AIDS, children being used as soldiers, corporate and political corruption, terrorism, and so on, and so on. It would be easy for so much evil to overwhelm us—and why many stick their heads in the sand and prefer to be entertained or distracted. They'd rather watch *Entertainment Tonight* than be troubled by learning more about the conflicts in the Middle East. In some ways I can't blame them, but on the other hand, since we are the ones equipped by heaven, are we really responsible Christians if we spend days on end without interceding in prayer?

As someone once said, "True love is talking with God about people; it's not talking with people about God." The call to love others as Christ loved us (John 15:12) has to start in prayer for others. But we don't have to take on the world—Jesus already did that for us, and He won! Our part is not to win a new victory over evil; it is to enter into the victory Jesus already won. We are, in essence, when we put on our prayer armor, putting on Christ's armor and entering with Him into intercession. As John "Praying" Hyde described, this joining in with the intercession of Jesus:

> ...affects our Father, for He looks upon Christ's prayer-life in us, and answers

accordingly. So that the answer is far "above all we can ask or think."...Christ's prayer life enters into us, and He prays in us. This is prayer in the Holy Spirit. Only thus can we pray without ceasing....No more working up a life of prayer and failing constantly. Jesus enters the boat, and the toiling ceases, and we are at the land whither we would be. Now, we need to be still before Him, so as to hear His voice and allow Him to pray in us—nay, allow Him to pour into our souls His over-flowing life of intercession, which means lit-erally: *face to face* meeting with God—real *union* and *communion*.[11]

Our task is not to worry. Yes, we are to be moved by the things we see and act to counteract them as best we can, but we must trust Jesus to lead us in prayer. We need to discipline ourselves to take time to pray, to prepare ourselves to enter the courtroom of heaven with our notes ready, our petition points listed, and our scriptural promises at hand, but once we get in there, we need to realize we are not the smart ones; Jesus is. We need to follow His lead. We need to listen to what He is praying and follow that line of thought. We are to open ourselves to the leadership and prayers of the Holy Spirit and focus where He directs us. Chances are there will be times He will give you one thing to pray through until you receive an answer in your spirit and know it is accomplished, and other times you go through your list and just spend time worshipping God.

As you do this, you will begin to find that you think about these things more often, not with an "oh, how awful!" attitude but a step-by-step process of how to walk out the answers for these problems as God plants ideas and nurtures them in your human spirit. You will find you have an attitude of being part of the solution rather than part of the problem. You will find yourself praying throughout the day and in whatever you are doing. This is the life God has called us to, and I believe it is the life really worth living—the life where your words and your deeds always agree.

SEVEN

IN WORD AND DEED

The Power of Aligning
Your Words With His

*If you abide in Me, and My words abide in you,
you will ask what you desire, and it shall be done
for you. By this My Father is glorified, that you
bear much fruit; so you will be My disciples.*

JOHN 15:7–8

*Sheer muscle and willpower don't make
anything happen. Every word I've spoken to
you is a Spirit-word, and so it is life-making.*

JOHN 6:63,
THE MESSAGE

THERE HAS BEEN a great deal written about the power of the spoken word over our environments and in the realm of the Spirit. If you have read any of my books—especially *Commanding Your Morning*—you will be familiar with many of these ideas (and if you haven't read that book, I would suggest that you do). In a very real sense, our words can shift the atmosphere around us. That is the power of intercessory prayer—and when we begin to speak in our daily lives the things that we pray in private, change happens. We need to realize that in a very tangible way, our words—*all of our words taken as a whole*—shape our realities.

Having taught this for some time, though, and in various places, I have seen people make two critical mistakes in understanding this truth. The first is they think they can speak out what they want to see happen but not truly surrender themselves to what is written in Scripture. Therefore they are not able to combine what they are saying with genuine faith. This would require them to invest more time studying God's Word so that more of His truth might be expressed in what they are saying. Secondly, they believe they can speak one way in prayer and another way in their day-to-day life, and their casual doubt, negativity, and unbelief won't affect what they are trying to stand in faith to see happen.

This is not how God intended it. Look, for example, at the Book of James, which addresses this issue from front to back. James warns us that the power of the tongue can too easily be used in the wrong way: "The tongue is so set among our members that it defiles the whole body, and sets on fire the course of nature" (James 3:6). He warns that we should be "swift to hear, slow to speak, slow to wrath" (James 1:19) because, since the tongue is so potent, we should never speak rashly or in anger. Why? Because what we say matters. What we say either edifies or poisons reality. At the same time, he tells us that the tongue has great power: "If you could find someone whose speech was perfectly true, you'd have a perfect person, in perfect control of life" (James 3:2, THE MESSAGE).

Now I know some of you have hang-ups about the word *perfect*. We have all heard the phrase "Nobody's perfect" so many times that it seems we should be able to reference it by chapter and verse. It's in the Book of Proverbs somewhere, isn't it? We have associated that word with brash arrogance, unattainable standards, or unreasonable expectations. But here in

James the word means "complete" or "mature."[1] In other words, someone who controls their tongue is a grown-up. They aren't ruled by the whims of childhood or adolescence. They don't throw temper tantrums on the floor. They are people with an aim and a purpose, focused on what is before them and aligning their words and their behaviors accordingly. This doesn't make them stiff or humorless either. It makes them intentional. They enjoy life. They enjoy their work. They enjoy their family. They enjoy their church. They are the type of people who are going somewhere—they happen to life; life doesn't just happen to them.

These are the type of people who don't throw out words as if they are some magical incantation that will bring them what they want. They use what they say to set their course. As James put it:

> A bit in the mouth of a horse controls the whole horse. A small rudder on a huge ship in the hands of a skilled captain sets a course in the face of the strongest winds. A word out of your mouth may seem of no account, but it can accomplish nearly anything—or destroy it!
>
> —JAMES 3:3–5, THE MESSAGE

Saying what we want—finding the Bible promises that support our desires or what we are interceding for and repeating them over and over—is relatively easy. Anyone can do that. And while that is a good thing to do, it is just the beginning. If you pull the bridle in one direction, but the rest of the horse does not go in that direction, what good is the bit? If you turn the rudder, but the ship's course stays the same, what good is trying to steer? No, it is only when the rest of our being turns to follow where we are directing by using the bit or the rudder that we actually change our lives or the lives of others through our prayers. Notice that the winds of life still blow, but when we use our tongue as the rudder of our actions and attitudes, the winds don't control where we are going; our words do.

As is written elsewhere in the Book of James, when we start to steer our lives by our words, we are slower to speak because we weigh everything that comes out of our mouths more conscientiously. We want to say things that truly represent what we mean and steer us in the right direction. We avoid speaking words that contradict our faith or our prayers. We don't belittle others or spit venom at them with the same mouths we use to praise God. As Scripture says,

"Does a spring send forth fresh water and bitter from the same opening? Can a fig tree, my brethren, bear olives, or a grapevine bear figs?" (James 3:11–12).

Not only that, but most important of all, our actions and attitudes begin to align with the direction our words are plotting out. We become "perfect" in word and deed as both line up to accomplish what we have been put on the earth to do. We become "integrous" at the most fundamental meaning of the word: there is a 100 percent alignment between who we are on the inside and who we are on the outside. Like steel or another alloy with high integrity, we are pure in motive and action through and through— and from that comes great strength.

Words are a spiritual force. They are containers shaped by our thoughts, intentions, and meaning— tools that chisel our lives and the lives of those around us into masterpieces. However, a sculptor who doesn't understand his tools, their purposes, and how to use them will not create anything worthy of display. In the same way we must study language and the Word of God to be able to pick the right word for the right occasion. We must both control and understand what is coming out of our mouths. You don't use a mallet to smooth edges and you can't refine detail with a jackhammer. It is the same whether we speak to God or to human beings. The words we choose in public or in our prayer closets matter more than you'd think.

Prayers work wonders, or they can create blunders if we don't understand the power of the spoken word. We are not trying to talk God into doing things He knows are bad ideas or that were birthed out of self-ishness. Prayer is not manipulation—and neither should our speech be, even if we are trying to per-suade our coworkers or convince children of some aim. When we go to God in prayer, we are reminding Him of His nature with praise, celebrating His promises with our petitions, and embracing His love as we speak on behalf of others. We are not twisting things so that we can get our own way. We are part-nering with Him in seeing His kingdom manifest.

Then, when we "leave" prayer, we go out into the world and speak the same way. We don't contradict the faith we expressed in prayer with doubt expressed to others. This is one expression of "praying without ceasing"—what we say to others throughout the day is in line with what we spoke to God about in private. And then our actions and attitudes follow suit. Our whole being focuses in on our goals and purposes with laser-like precision. Not only that, but we also begin to affect the atmosphere wherever we go. It is like we walk around in an ever-enlarging cloud of the kingdom of God, and the more places we go and the more consistent we are in aligning our words and actions with the Word and will of God, the bigger that cloud grows around us and over those we interact with each day.

When how we live, who we are, and what we say all line up, it is a powerful force for good. As E. M. Bounds put it in his book *The Necessity of Prayer*:

> Prayer is based on character. What we are with God gauges our influence with Him. It was the inner character, not the outward seeming, of such men as Abraham, Job, David, Moses and all others, who had such great influence with God in the days of old. And, today, it is not so much our words, as what we really are, which weighs with God. Conduct affects character, of course, and counts for much in our praying. At the same time, character affects conduct to a far greater extent, and has a superior influence over prayer. Our inner life not only gives colour to our praying, but body, as well. Bad living means bad

praying and, in the end, no praying at all. We pray feebly because we live feebly. The stream of prayer cannot rise higher than the fountain of living. The force of the inner chamber is made up of the energy which flows from the confluent streams of living. And the weakness of living grows out of the shallowness and shoddiness of character.

Feebleness of living reflects its debility and langour in the praying hours. We simply cannot talk to God, strongly, intimately, and confidently unless we are living for Him, faithfully and truly. The prayer-closet cannot become sanctified unto God, when the life is alien to His precepts and purpose. We must learn this lesson well—that righteous character and Christlike conduct give us a peculiar and preferential standing in prayer before God.[2]

WORDS CREATE OUR WORLD

All of our words begin with thoughts resulting from nucleic acids and biochemical impulses firing between synapsis in our brains. These build dendrite clusters—or branching pathways—that create paradigms—or frameworks within which we define the elements and experiences of our world. As we process information, our thoughts produce vibrations in our vocal cords that find expression through the phenomena of speech. To see permanent change, you must have a permanent paradigm shift. You don't create a path through a forest by taking a new route each time to cross it. You have to be consistent in your words, prayers, and actions. As we are focused and intentional in thought and speech, we permanently alter our perceptions and our habits, and thus align our actions with what we are believing for in prayer, creating a lifestyle of godliness and power.

Hebrews 11:3 tells us, "By faith we understand that the worlds were framed by the word of God, so that the things which are seen were not made of things which are visible." James 2:17 states, "Faith by itself, if it does not have works [actions], is dead." Your expectations, thoughts, and beliefs manifest in your speech and change the things around you. Though it is to a lesser degree, it is the same principle by which God spoke the world into being in Genesis chapter 1. He formed ideas of what He wanted, infused those meanings into words, spoke them into the nothingness, and the universe we live in today was formed.

He is the God who "calls into being that which does not exist" (Rom. 4:17, NAS). This is the way that thoughts become things. You are, literally, creating reality by your prayers and your words. You are doing it every day with the thoughts you are thinking, the words you are speaking, and the prayers that, as a result, you are praying.

While it remains true that the key to seeing everything is to first believe it, there is, in fact, scientific evidence to support the concept that your words shape your own world. Seeing does not always produce believing, but believing will produce seeing.

Some of the best scientific evidence behind the concept that you create your own reality can be seen through the study of electrons. Electrons are a main component (some even say they are the "building blocks") of all matter. Electrons are not particles that sometimes become waves, nor are they waves that sometimes become particles. Instead, in a stimulus-free environment, electrons exist in a state of potential until they are interacted with. Electrons are in a sense everything and nothing, wave and particle at the same time. They are in a state of potential until you or something else observes/interacts with them. Observation is not the most important thing, however, that dictates the form electrons take. The expectation (thought) of the observer is.

This is one conclusion that has been drawn as the result of the "double-slit experiment." During this experiment scientists placed an electron cannon in a stimulus-free chamber. It was then aimed at a wall with two slits in it. Recording the final landing points of the electrons after they passed through the slits was another wall. The cannon fired electrons at the first wall one at a time but very rapidly, much the same as a machine gun fires bullets. If a machine gun were to be fired at a wall with two slits, the bullets would produce a pattern of bullet holes on the second wall that corresponds to the diameters of the two slits on the first wall. Therefore it was widely thought that the electron cannon would create the same results. They should, in a sense, have formed two roughly rectangular patterns (a slightly larger outline of each slit) on the second wall.

However, that is not what happened in the double-slit experiment. While some of the electrons in the double-slit experiment hit the first wall and were absorbed by it, most of the electrons instead made impressions all over the second wall, and these impressions did not correspond with the slits at all;

instead they formed wave patterns on the second wall. Scientists then positioned a photon emitter to fire a photon at each electron as it traveled toward the two slits. They found that doing this changed the results of the double-slit experiment. When the photons collided with each electron before they passed through one of the two slits, the electrons made it through one of the two slits only to land on the second wall in the machine-gun bullet pattern they expected to see the first time. This experiment has been repeated several times, and the results challenge physicists even today. The experiment boldly points to the truth that through interaction via observation and expectation, you are creating the very form that matter takes.

All matter that you see in this physical dimension is simply energy vibrating in such a way that it takes on static properties. When it does this, you perceive things as being solid. Matter is, however, totally unsubstantial. Nearly 99 percent of an atom (which makes up all the matter there is) is actually "empty space." That means that through our positive confessions of faith or expectations we can influence how the world around us takes form. Prayer, in essence, is our opportunity to speak the language of change.

Thus intercession becomes a lifestyle.

As you pray and decree a thing, the meaning, purpose, and faith invested in your words travel at a frequency affecting anything and everything that flows along its path at a subatomic level. In this light, thoughts are, in fact, things. Thoughts are given vitality by your belief, attitudes, and emotions. They are activated by the law of focused attention. Whatever you give your consideration to—whatever you focus on—grows in terms of relevance, importance, and significance. Words, whether positive or negative, are a powerful, driving force. Jesus said, "The words that I speak to you are spirit, and they are life" (John 6:63). In order to express itself, your faith must attach itself to an image formed by your words so that the outward manifestation has a pattern after which to form.

How can we develop the faith to shatter strongholds, overcome hardship, defy odds, and believe God for the impossible? How can we develop the courage to believe that the thoughts that emanate from the mind of God will manifest in reality?

God knows the end from the beginning, and if we will spend time in prayer listening for His guidance, He will share it with us. His plans and purposes for the earth can come to pass only through those with legal jurisdiction on our planet. We are the key. But it takes faith. You must develop the courage and faith to take the risk to pull away, pray, and then sit quietly and wait for God to answer. This is how we operate in the realm of faith. This is how we bring our thoughts, ideas, dreams, and visions to pass.

An Important Note

As we pray for others in this way and speak out God's Word over our atmospheres, we need to remember that just as God respects the jurisdiction each of us has over our own lives and choices, we must have the same respect for those we are praying for. We should be praying that God opens their eyes so that they can see the truth and make the right choices for themselves (just as God does for each of us who call on His name), not that God will make those we are praying for do this or that. After all, Jesus has already done everything He needs to do to see a person is saved—Christ never has to go back to the cross and die again—but once He was done, He didn't force that decision on anyone. He left it to each of us to decide on our own to accept His free gift of salvation or not. In His great love He will not even force heaven upon any of us.

That is why it is important to remember that this is not some kind of magical thinking or that speaking scriptures out over our situations is like something out of the Harry Potter series. We are not manipulating people, atmospheres, or events to get what we want; we are speaking out God's will over them, and His laws and promises to enforce that will. Once again, intercession is not manipulation; it is turning on the light so those stumbling in the dark can finally find their ways to the door for themselves. Remember, Esther didn't just petition that the Jews would be saved—she requested they be armed and equipped to fend for themselves.

Intercession takes mental strength and spiritual fortitude, which are developed in the same way your natural strength is. You must "exercise" regularly. You must meditate on the meaning of your and God's words night and day. Your mind-set and beliefs must align with your words and behaviors. To take your thoughts to the next level—to the creation of witty ideas and innovative inventions—practice thinking in terms of possibilities over the next several weeks. Believe the best and speak according to those beliefs until it becomes a habit. When you believe you can influence the world through prayer—when you are able to open your mind to the miraculous and expect better outcomes—then you will begin to see change come to pass. This will drive your work, and God will show you answers and bless the things you set your hand to do.

> Prayer is striking the winning blow at the concealed enemy. Service is gathering up the results of that blow among the men we see and touch.[3]
>
> —S. D. GORDON

> God's Word is an indispensable weapon. In the same way, prayer is essential in this ongoing warfare. Pray hard and long. Pray for your brothers and sisters. Keep your eyes open. Keep each other's spirits up so that no one falls behind or drops out.
>
> —EPHESIANS 6:17–18, THE MESSAGE

EIGHT

LET JUSTICE ROLL DOWN

Let Freedom Ring

But let justice roll down like waters and
righteousness like an ever-flowing stream.

AMOS 5:24, NAS

He wants not only us but everyone saved, you
know, everyone to get to know the truth we've
learned: that there's one God and only one,
and one Priest-Mediator between God and
us—Jesus, who offered himself in exchange for
everyone held captive by sin, to set them all free.

1 TIMOTHY 2:4–6,
THE MESSAGE

WHEN MARTIN LUTHER King Jr. quoted Amos 5:24 in his "I Have a Dream" speech, he did not do so lightly. To him justice was a central part of the nature of God. I like how I once heard Cornel West describe it: "Justice is what love looks like in public." Love indeed—and no one should be better examples of that than those of us who follow Jesus.

A lot of people mistake *justice* as retribution or revenge. They think of taking someone to court and "getting even" for what that person took or damaged. Just look at some of the courtroom reality shows that are on afternoon TV, and you will see this quickly. People are trying to get even for something someone did to them.

Christianity is different, however. In Christ's ideal, no one would ever have to take someone else to court—we would be able to work it out on our own between the two parties.

> Agree with your adversary quickly, while you are on the way with him, lest your adversary deliver you to the judge, the judge hand you over to the officer, and you are thrown into prison. Assuredly, I say to you, you will by no

means get out of there till you have paid the last penny.

—Matthew 5:25–26

Furthermore, God tells us, "Vengeance is Mine, I will repay" (Rom. 12:19). And Jesus put it this way: "Bless those who curse you, and pray for those who spitefully use you" (Luke 6:28). In fact, God seems to have a very different picture of justice than many of us do.

Justice Is Served

One of the first acts of justice we see doled out after the cross is on a persecutor of the early church and at least an accomplice to murder. He was a legalist to his very bones and persecuted the followers of Jesus with what he thought was a holy vengeance. His name? Saul of Tarsus.

The Book of Acts tells us that Saul stood by and held the coats of the men who stoned Stephen to death so that they wouldn't get splattered with blood. In Acts chapter 9 he is on his way to Damascus with letters authorizing him to extradite in chains to Jerusalem any Christians he found there. God looked down at this bloodthirsty zealot, and you know what

He saw? A man that His Son had given His life for. So rather than send down a lightning bolt to strike him dead, He sent Jesus.

So Jesus appears before Paul with such a striking brilliance that it knocks him off his horse and blinds him. There is no beating around the bush either. Jesus gets straight to the point. "Saul, Saul," He says (I imagine Him shaking His head), "why are you persecuting Me?"[1] (Notice that Jesus doesn't ask, "Why are you persecuting My followers?" For Him, this is very personal.)

Saul responds, "Who are You, Lord?"

"I am Jesus, whom you are persecuting. It is hard for you to kick against the goads."

Now, as a bit of an aside, I find that a very interesting comment: "It is hard to kick against the goads." A goad is something used to help a herd of cattle or sheep know the right way to go. The "right way," of course, is the direction the cowhands or shepherds want the animals to go. It was Jesus's way of telling Saul, as they would on the beaches of California, "Dude, you're going the wrong way!" This again implies that the Shepherd had a different plan for this particular sheep's life. Here Jesus is trying to direct Saul of Tarsus to become Paul the apostle, and

Saul is fighting Him with everything he has. Jesus tries to push him in one direction, and Saul turns and attacks the very people Jesus sent into his life to try to help him.

So, Jesus decides to corner him Himself. Once Jesus shows up in someone's life, it has a significant way of changing things.

Like a wise man, once Jesus shows up, Saul realizes his mistakes. He instantly connects all the dots of his life—all the places God has tried to reach out to him with the truth, all the people God put in his life to teach him about His true nature—and realizes it is time to change. Now, in that instant, not the next day or the next week, Saul instantly has a change of heart. "Lord, what do You want me to do?"

Though he uses the same word—"Lord"—in the two times he speaks here, I think each time means something very different. The first time he is talking to an authority, like the lord of a manor or estate; the second time he is talking to his Lord and Savior. In a flash Saul's heart is changed. As he later described it: "Old things have passed away; behold, all things have become new" (2 Cor. 5:17). After all, wasn't it Saul (Paul) who wrote, "If you confess with your mouth the Lord Jesus and believe in your heart that God has raised Him from the dead, you will be saved" (Rom. 10:9)? He knew the power of proclaiming Jesus as Lord.

Then Jesus answered, "Arise and go into the city, and you will be told what you must do."

Now Jesus didn't just stop Saul in his tracks. He changed him. He took a tool in the hand of the devil who was trying to wipe Christianity from the earth before it was even called Christianity, and He turned it into the greatest proponent and catalyst for Christianity the world has ever known. This is the guy, after all, who wrote about three-quarters of the New Testament! And he didn't even walk with Jesus—had he been there, he probably would have been one of the ones crying out "Crucify Him! Crucify Him!"

In a world where all sin has been paid for once and for all through the cross, justice is no longer retribution. God isn't going to kill Saul for killing Stephen; instead He is going to infect him with the zeal Stephen had. And He is going to make him ten times the evangelist that Stephen ever was!

Saul (Paul) knew the severity of this too. This is why he wrote the following—quoting Proverbs

25:21–22—about justice in the book of Romans, the cornerstone letter of everything he ever wrote:

> "If your enemy is hungry, feed him;
> If he is thirsty, give him a drink;
> For in so doing you will heap coals of fire on
>   his head."
> Do not be overcome by evil, but overcome
>   evil with good.
>
> —ROMANS 12:20–21

INTERCESSION MEANS TRANSFORMATION

When we intercede for the persecuted, the oppressed, and the exploited, we need to remember to pray as well for their persecutors, their oppressors, and those who are exploiting them. We need to pray that the full "penalty" of heaven rains down on their heads just as it did on Saul as he was on his way to Damascus.

There will be no stopping these crimes without a change of heart for the criminals. If you have read my book *The Prayer Warrior's Way*, it is possible you will remember the story of John Newton, who became a critical supporter of the abolitionist movement in Great Britain along with William

Wilberforce. Together with others these men fought to end slavery throughout the British Empire, and they succeeded some three decades before the Civil War tore the United States apart over the same issue. Why was Newton's help so significant? Because he had been the captain of a slave ship. He himself had performed the atrocities they were working to end. He knew the inhumanity of the trade because it had threatened to take his very humanity from him. But, like Paul, John Newton met Jesus, and everything changed. John learned about the "Amazing Grace" of God and wrote about it in what is perhaps the most transcendent and greatest hymn ever written.

An interesting thing about that song is that it is not written using the eight-note scale we are used to in the West, but the pentatonic (five-note) scale that is native to Africa and throughout African American spirituals. You can literally play the song only using the black keys on a piano keyboard. It is quite possibly a melody that rose up through the decking of one of Newton's ships as the slaves below sang and tried to cheer themselves even in the worst of conditions. Newton used it as the backbone of his song and a battle cry for setting all slaves, everywhere, free.

For every slave saved, there is a slave saved; but

for every slaver saved, thousands might be saved! We cannot neglect to pray for the perpetrators as well as the exploited. We must pray for changed hearts on both sides of these crimes, for there is no advocate like a reformed criminal.

And people must be praying like this somewhere, for throughout the Arab world people approach churches on almost a daily basis saying they had a dream the night before and they want to know, "Who is this Jesus?" This has even happened to terrorists. God is changing hearts. God is showing up in new ways. As Charles Finney expressed it in his *Lectures on Revival*:

> O, for a praying church! I once knew a minister who had a revival fourteen winters in succession. I did not know how to account for it, till I saw one of his members get up in a prayer meeting, and make a confession. "Brethren," said he, "I have been long in the habit of praying every Saturday night till after midnight, for the descent of the Holy Ghost among us. And now, brethren," and he began to weep, "I confess that I have neglected it for two or three weeks." The secret was out. That minister had a praying church....Now, will

not you…throw yourselves into this work, and bear this burden, and give yourselves to prayer, till God shall pour out His blessing upon us?[2]

Brothers and sisters, we have work to do, but it is far from a work without rewards. Intercessory prayer—and the process of becoming a part of the answer to those prayers—is about as great an adventure as there is on this planet. Embrace it. Dare to ask God for great things. Be consistent in it. Learn and grow. And always let the Spirit of God lead you at all times, for:

> When the Spirit of truth comes, he will guide you into all truth. He will not speak on his own but will tell you what he has heard. He will tell you about the future. He will bring me glory by telling you whatever he receives from me. All that belongs to the Father is mine; this is why I said, "The Spirit will tell you whatever he receives from me."
> —JOHN 16:13–15, NLT

PULLING IT ALL TOGETHER

We must become such a people of prayer. It is impossible to be in true relationship with God and not have prayer and intercession be a significant part of your life. It is the life Jesus lived when He walked the earth. It is the very challenge Jesus laid down to His own disciples:

> This is My commandment, that you love one another as I have loved you. Greater love has no one than this, than to lay down one's life for his friends. You are My friends if you do whatever I command you. No longer do I call you servants, for a servant does not know what his master is doing; but I have called you friends, for all things that I heard from My Father I have made known to you.
>
> —JOHN 15:12–15

While God so loved the world that He gave His only Son, His only Son so loved the world that He has never stopped praying for us since the moment He returned to the Father's right hand. If we are going to love as He loved, then intercession has to be part of who we are. Jesus didn't just challenge, though; He also made a promise. If we joined Him in this ministry, we wouldn't be servants blindly going along and not knowing the right decisions to make or the right things to ask of the Father—we would be His friends, like faithful Abraham, and we would know what God was up to on the earth. For when we join with the Spirit of God in prayer, we don't just stand before the throne of heaven to plead our cases; we gain access to godly insight and revelation of what and how to pray.

But as I said earlier, the school of prayer isn't really found in books; it is found in practice. (Though I believe books like this one can help!) You learn as you go, and depth of prayer is never touched until you are willing to first wade out into the shallows. You need a plan and strategy to tackle it from day one—baby steps.

That is why I have included a prayer outline in Appendix B in the back of this book either for you to use as is or for you to adapt with your own Scripture verses and prompts. While many of my other books have prayers in the back filled with declarations and decrees for you to proclaim over your own life, I felt led to do something different with this book. Since you are now praying for others, you need reminders of what to pray for, rather than statements to repeat, and passages that will encourage your faith and boldness in prayer before the throne of grace and as you ask the Holy Spirit what you should be praying. Then you need to develop your prayer routine.

Go back to chapter 5 and work through the instructions there to find the names of government officials, local pastors, and so forth. Add any other names God puts on your heart. Write them in Appendix B, or as I suggested before, create your own computer, smartphone, or tablet document so it can be easily updated. Print it out and stick it in your purse, briefcase, or Bible, where it will be handy whenever you feel led to pray.

Now determine a time you are going to pray regularly, even if it is just ten to fifteen minutes each morning, at noon, or before you go to sleep at night. (Daniel, who had great success in his secular world, prayed during all three!) It is a good idea to start on a Saturday when you are not constrained by time or perhaps a Sunday morning right after you wake up and before you start getting ready for church. Find a quiet place.

Set the atmosphere by putting on some praise music to play softly in the background and cut down outside noise, or turn on the live Web feed from the prayer room at the International House of Prayer in Kansas City through their website at www.ihopkc .org. It is also great to plug into this when IHOP prays for specific topics that are also on your heart— such as inner-city missions and churches or sex trafficking. Again, check their website for when these happen. If you feel led to, sing and praise God for a time. Play an instrument instead of putting on music. Do whatever you feel you should do to uplift your Lord and Savior and welcome His presence.

Then open to Appendix B (or you prayer sheet or smartphone or tablet document) and begin praying. You may want to start by just reading over and meditating on the scriptures in the outline and the names of God and what they mean. Ask God about them, then sit silently and listen for His response. Tell God how much you appreciate who He is and what He has done for you. Don't be in a hurry. Simply sit and welcome the presence of God.

As you get to the section entitled "Petitions, Supplication, Intercessions," read through the list and pray whatever comes to mind for each person one by one. After you have prayed what you know to pray, ask the Holy Spirit what He would have you pray. As Paul said, "I will pray with the spirit, and I will also pray with the understanding [his mind]. I will sing with the spirit, and I will also sing with the understanding" (1 Cor. 14:15). About this process in intercession, Oswald Chambers advised:

> It is not that we bring God into touch with our minds, but that we rouse ourselves until God is able to convey His mind to us about the one for whom we intercede.
>
> Is Jesus Christ seeing of the travail of His soul in us? He cannot unless we are so identified with Himself that we are roused up to get His view about the people for whom we pray. May we learn to intercede so whole-heartedly that Jesus Christ will be abundantly satisfied with us as intercessors.[3]

Repeat this process for every person on the list. Write down notes or Scripture references for things that come to your mind as you pray. Don't just quote the scriptures, but turn them into prayers, taking out the pronouns and putting in the names of the people you are praying for. For example, if you were going to the Ephesians chapter 1 prayer for President Barak Obama, it would go something like this:

I pray that You, the God of our Lord Jesus Christ, the Father of glory, would give unto President Obama the spirit of wisdom and revelation in the knowledge of Your Son, Jesus; that the eyes of his understanding would be enlightened; that the president would know what is the hope of Your calling for his life, what are the riches of the glory of Your inheritance in the saints, and what is the exceeding greatness of Your power toward all of us who believe.[4]

Write—or type—these out if you need to so that you can read through them word for word and not get distracted by having to replace words or change their wordings to fit on the fly. (You can also find resources, like the book *Prayers That Avail Much*, that are scriptural prayers for different topics that have blanks in them so you can easily insert names and pronouns.) Do the same for the scriptures you read as personal petitions and for each topic for the rest of the outline, working your way through to the end. As you prepare to finish, go back into praise and worship and thank God that He is already answering your prayers.

When you say "Amen," remember that *amen* means, "Let it be so," not "good-bye for now." You are not "signing off" to visit with God again the next day; you are signing your prayers with your faith. It is like signing your name to a letter you were writing a congressman or on a petition. You are saying, "This is what I believe. This is why I believe it. These are the promises in Your Word for why it should come to pass. Let it be so, in the name of Jesus."

While I think it is a good idea to go through the entire outline the first time you do this, it is tough in our modern world to spend the time it would take for this every day, so have some grace for yourself. As I said before, I want to you to have a burden to pray (what they used to call the prompting from within their hearts that they should pray for this issue or that person), but I don't want prayer to be a burden on you—a yoke of legalism or duty. There should be no guilt for missing a day or for not having the time to go through the entire outline each time you look at it. Pick and choose from it as you see fit. Replace the verses that don't speak to you. Skim some parts, and spend more time in others as you feel led by the Spirit. Let the Holy Spirit be your guide in this—what I have given you here is just a guideline to use as God leads you to use it.

What is important is that you develop a lifestyle where prayer is central to everything you do. Moses was known as the humblest man who walked the earth, because whenever he faced an issue, he would simply fall to his face right where he was and start praying. We should feel free to do the same when we meet things throughout our days (though I think you should really be led by the Holy Spirit if you are going to fall to your face in your workplace or on the street to start praying!). We need to be a people willing to turn off the TV and spend an evening in prayer and praise. We need to let God know we are available when He needs us to intercede. We need to let the desire to pray grow in us without letting it become a legalistic yoke of bondage. As Scripture tells us, Jesus is waiting to sit and visit with us at all times:

> Behold, I stand at the door and knock. If anyone hears My voice and opens the door, I will come in to him and dine with him, and he with Me. To him who overcomes I will grant to sit with Me on My throne, as I also

overcame and sat down with My Father on
His throne.

—REVELATION 3:20–21

As you develop prayer in your own life in this way,
look for as many outside supports as you can. Are
there prayer groups at your church that you can join,
or is your church open to you forming one? Meeting
regularly with others to intercede, especially for specific topics or concerns, is a powerful support for a
life and culture of prayer. Is there a 24/7 prayer room
in your community where you can sign up for a shift
a couple times a week? It greatly decreases distractions to have a place to go and pray that is set aside
for just that purpose. Again, perhaps your church is
open to creating such a room or is open for people
to go into the main auditorium at certain hours of
the day to pray. Pursue this particularly if you are
having trouble carving out quiet, undisrupted time
for prayer at home. Take advantage of whatever
resources strengthen your prayer times, and as you
grow, create such resources for others in your area
to support the culture of prayer in your community.

God Has Extended
His Scepter to You

When Esther did finally make her entry before King Ahasuerus, her preparation was not in vain. The king extended his scepter to her and honored her request to come and dine with her. Esther set a lavish table before her king and was glad to converse with him, showing no hint that she needed to rush through things so she could get to something else or that she was concerned with doing anything other than being in his presence. When he asked her for her petition at the end of the time together, she invited him to another evening with her. It was spending time with him that she wanted to show was important, not just getting an answer to whatever her petition was.

When she did finally present her petition, the king not only granted it once, but twice, extending the right to the Jewish people to arm themselves, defend themselves, and then make a spoil of their enemies, making sure it would be a long time before they were challenged again.

The life of prayer is a life of standing for and with others, just as Jesus is doing at this very minute. We focus on empowering others and seeing God's kingdom established in their lives. We reach out with the power and wisdom of God to lift people out of the traps evil has set for them and find satisfaction and fulfillment in the presence of God. This is the life of seeing God's justice roll down, changing the hearts of the abusers and healing the abused.

Do not let it be said of our generation that when God looked for someone to stand in the gap for an issue, He could find no one willing do it. All those who say we belong to Christ should be willing to stand in the place—and need to do so regularly. God Himself issued the invitation in Jeremiah 33:3: "Call to Me, and I will answer you, and show you great and mighty things, which you do not know."

Oh, there is so much to accomplish, but there are also so many resources available to us if we would trust God to reveal them to us. Pursue Him in prayer and lift up the nations to Him that His will might be done in them just as they are in heaven. Justice always begins with a people who will stand for it and not be denied. Enter before our King and demand His justice be realized.

The world, after all, is waiting for the sons and daughters of God to manifest. May we be that people for a world that still so needs our Savior.

ORGANIZATIONS FOR JUSTICE AND FREEDOM

THE FOLLOWING ORGANIZATIONS are just a few of many. The ones I have listed are those that friends, staff members, or partners have suggested from the organizations they support. I urge you to check out their websites or do a general search on issues that touch your heart and see where God inspires you to connect, help, and pray.

Helping orphans

River's Promise
www.riverspromise.org
888.285.4669

World Vision
www.worldvision.org
888.511.6443

Poverty and AIDS

One

www.one.org

202.495.2700

The needy and homeless

The Salvation Army

www.salvationarmyusa.org

Put in your zip code to find their facilities in your area.

The prayer room movement

24-7 Prayer

www.24-7prayer.com

http://24-7prayer.us

816.931.2841

The International House of Prayer

www.ihopkc.org

816.763.0200

Religious freedom

Open Doors

www.opendoorsusa.org

888.524.2535 (888-5-BIBLE-5)

The Voice of the Martyrs
www.persecution.com
877.337.0302

Slavery and sex trafficking

Exodus Cry
www.exoduscry.com
816.398.7490

iEmpathize
www.iempathize.com
303.625.4074

Love146
www.Love146.org
203.772.4420

Not For Sale
www.notforsalecampaign.org
650.560.9990

AN EXAMPLE OF A PRAYER GUIDE FOR PRAYING THE DISCIPLE'S PRAYER

PRAISE

"Our Father who art in heaven…"

We are His children by virtue of:

+ His blood

But now in Christ Jesus you who once were far off have been brought near by the blood of Christ.

—EPHESIANS 2:13

+ His Spirit

For the law of the Spirit of life in Christ Jesus has made me free from the law of sin and death….For as many as are led by the Spirit of God, these are sons of God.

—ROMANS 8:2, 14

* Our faith

For you are all sons of God through faith in Christ Jesus.
—Galatians 3:26

"Hallowed be Your name."

His names are covenant names:

* *El Elyon*: The God Most High

"Blessed be Abram of God Most High, possessor of heaven and earth; and blessed be God Most High, who has delivered your enemies into your hand." And he gave him a tithe of all.
—Genesis 14:19–20

And he [the demon] cried out with a loud voice and said, "What have I to do with You, Jesus, Son of the Most High God? I implore You by God that You do not torment me."
—Mark 5:7

* *El Shaddai*: God Almighty

When Abram was ninety-nine years old, the Lord appeared to Abram and said to him, "I am Almighty God; walk before Me and be blameless."

—Genesis 17:1

"I am the Alpha and the Omega, the Beginning and the End," says the Lord, "who is and who was and who is to come, the Almighty."

—Revelation 1:8

• *El Olam*: The Everlasting God

Then Abraham planted a tamarisk tree in Beersheba, and there called on the name of the Lord, the Everlasting God.

—Genesis 21:33

Jesus Christ is the same yesterday, today, and forever.

—Hebrews 13:8

• *Jehovah Jireh*: The Lord's Provision Shall Be Seen

And Abraham called the name of the place, The-Lord-Will-Provide; as it is said to this day, "In the Mount of The Lord it shall be provided."

—Genesis 22:14

God is able to make all grace abound toward you, that you, always having all sufficiency in all things, may have an abundance for every good work.

—2 CORINTHIANS 9:8

+ *Jehovah Rophe*: God Heals

If you diligently heed the voice of the LORD your God and do what is right in His sight, give ear to His commandments and keep all His statutes, I will put none of the diseases on you which I have brought on the Egyptians. For I am the LORD who heals you.

—EXODUS 15:26

Who Himself bore our sins in His own body on the tree, that we, having died to sins, might live for righteousness—by whose stripes you were healed.

—1 PETER 2:24

+ *Jehovah Nissi*: God My Banner

Moses built an altar and called its name, The-Lord-Is-My-Banner; for he said, "Because the LORD has sworn: the LORD will have war with Amalek from generation to generation."

—EXODUS 17:15–16

Thanks be to God, who gives us the victory through our Lord Jesus Christ.

—1 CORINTHIANS 15:57

+ *Jehovah M'kaddesh*: The Lord Who Sanctifies

Speak also to the children of Israel, saying: "Surely My Sabbaths you shall keep, for it is a sign between Me and you throughout your generations, that you may know that I am the LORD who sanctifies you."

—EXODUS 31:13

Therefore do not be ashamed of the testimony of our Lord, nor of me His prisoner, but share with me in the sufferings for the gospel according to the power of God, who has saved us and called us with a holy calling, not according to our works, but according to His own purpose and grace which was given to us in Christ Jesus before time began.

—2 TIMOTHY 1:8–9

+ *Jehovah Shalom*: The Lord Is Peace

So Gideon built an altar there to the LORD, and called it The-LORD-Is-Peace.

—JUDGES 6:24

Be anxious for nothing, but in everything by prayer and supplication, with thanksgiving, let your requests be made known to God; and the peace of God, which surpasses all understanding, will guard your hearts and minds through Christ Jesus.

—PHILIPPIANS 4:6–7

+ *Jehovah Sabaoth*: The Lord of Hosts

This man went up from his city yearly to worship and sacrifice to the LORD of hosts in Shiloh.

—1 SAMUEL 1:3

Or do you think that I cannot now pray to My Father, and He will provide Me with more than twelve legions of angels?

—MATTHEW 26:53

• *Jehovah Rohi*: The Lord My Shepherd

The Lord is my shepherd; I shall not want. He makes me to lie down in green pastures; He leads me beside the still waters. He restores my soul; He leads me in the paths of righteousness for His name's sake. Yea, though I walk through the valley of the shadow of death, I will fear no evil; for You are with me; Your rod and Your staff, they comfort me. You prepare a table before me in the presence of my enemies; You anoint my head with oil; my cup runs over. Surely goodness and mercy shall follow me all the days of my life; and I will dwell in the house of the Lord forever.

—Psalm 23:1–6

When he brings out his own sheep, he goes before them; and the sheep follow him, for they know his voice.

—John 10:4

• *Jehovah Tsidkenu*: God Our Righteousness

In His days Judah will be saved, and Israel will dwell safely; now this is His name by

which He will be called: THE LORD OUR
RIGHTEOUSNESS.

—JEREMIAH 23:6

For He made Him who knew no sin to be sin
for us, that we might become the righteousness of God in Him.

—2 CORINTHIANS 5:21

+ *Jehovah Shammah*: The Lord Is Present

All the way around shall be eighteen thousand cubits; and the name of the city from
that day shall be: THE LORD IS THERE.

—EZEKIEL 48:35

Let your conduct be without covetousness;
be content with such things as you have. For
He Himself has said, "I will never leave you
nor forsake you." So we may boldly say: "The
LORD is my helper; I will not fear. What can
man do to me?"

—HEBREWS 13:5–6

SANCTIFICATION, SUPPLICATIONS, INTERCESSIONS

"Your kingdom come. Your will be done on earth as it is in heaven."

> Therefore I exhort first of all that supplications, prayers, intercessions, and giving of thanks be made for all men, for kings and all who are in authority, that we may lead a quiet and peaceable life in all godliness and reverence. For this is good and acceptable in the sight of God our Savior.
>
> —1 TIMOTHY 2:1–3

+ The government[1]

+ President and spouse

> The king's heart is in the hand of the LORD, like the rivers of water; He turns it wherever He wishes.
>
> —PROVERBS 21:1

+ Vice president and spouse

+ Congress

+ State senators

- District representatives
- State officials, police, government workers
- Governor
- Senator to the state assembly
- Representative to the state assembly
- County commissioners
- Mayor
- Pastors in your area
- Other ministries or organizations
- Your family
- Your friends
- Others you feel led to pray for
- Peace in Israel

Personal Petitions

"Give us this day our daily bread."

- Finances: put God first

Seek first the kingdom of God and His righteousness, and all these things shall be added to you.

—MATTHEW 6:33

Beloved, I pray that you may prosper in all things and be in health, just as your soul prospers.

—3 JOHN 2

My God shall supply all your need according to His riches in glory by Christ Jesus.

—PHILIPPIANS 4:19

✦   Tithing

"Bring all the tithes into the storehouse, that there may be food in My house, and try Me now in this," says the LORD of hosts, "if I will not open for you the windows of heaven and pour out for you such blessing that there will not be room enough to receive it.

"And I will rebuke the devourer for your sakes, so that he will not destroy the fruit of your ground, nor shall the vine fail to bear fruit for you in the field," says the LORD of hosts; "and all nations will call you blessed,

for you will be a delightful land," says the
LORD of hosts.

—MALACHI 3:10–12

+ Giving

But this I say: He who sows sparingly will
also reap sparingly, and he who sows bountifully will also reap bountifully. So let each
one give as he purposes in his heart, not
grudgingly or of necessity; for God loves a
cheerful giver. And God is able to make all
grace abound toward you, that you, always
having all sufficiency in all things, may have
an abundance for every good work.

—2 CORINTHIANS 9:6–8

The LORD will command the blessing on you
in your storehouses and in all to which you
set your hand, and He will bless you in the
land which the LORD your God is giving you.

—DEUTERONOMY 28:8

Godliness with contentment is great gain.

—1 TIMOTHY 6:6

Make sure that your character is free from the
love of money, being content with what you

have; for He Himself has said, "I will never desert you, nor will I ever forsake you," so that we confidently say, "The Lord is my helper, I will not be afraid. What will man do to me?"

—Hebrews 13:5–6, nas

+ Health and healing

But He was wounded for our transgressions, He was bruised for our iniquities; the chastisement for our peace was upon Him, and by His stripes we are healed. All we like sheep have gone astray; we have turned, every one, to his own way; and the Lord has laid on Him the iniquity of us all.

—Isaiah 53:5–6

But if the Spirit of Him who raised Jesus from the dead dwells in you, He who raised Christ from the dead will also give life to your mortal bodies through His Spirit who dwells in you.

—Romans 8:11

My son, give attention to my words; incline your ear to my sayings. Do not let them depart from your eyes; keep them in the midst of your heart; for they are life to those who find them, and health to all their flesh. Keep your heart with all diligence, for out of it spring the issues of life.

—Proverbs 4:20–23

Sanctification

"And forgive us our debts, as we forgive our debtors."

* Ask forgiveness.

Whoever has been born of God does not sin, for His seed remains in him; and he cannot sin, because he has been born of God.

—1 John 3:9

* Forgive and release others
* Set your will to walk in forgiveness throughout the day

"And do not lead us into temptation, but deliver us from the evil one."

* Put on the full armor of God (Eph. 6:14–17).

  » Loins girt about with truth

- » Breastplate of righteousness
- » Feet shod with the readiness of the gospel of peace
- » Shield of faith
- » Helmet of salvation
- » Sword of the Spirit which is the Word of God

- Pray a hedge of protection.

He who dwells in the secret place of the Most High shall abide under the shadow of the Almighty. I will say of the LORD, "He is my refuge and my fortress; my God, in Him I will trust."…

"Because he has set his love upon Me, therefore I will deliver him; I will set him on high, because he has known My name. He shall call upon Me, and I will answer him; I will be with him in trouble; I will deliver him and honor him. With long life I will satisfy him, and show him My salvation."

—PSALM 91:1–2, 14–16

Praise

"For Yours is the kingdom and the power and the glory forever."

+ Thank Him for the answers to your prayers.

Now this is the confidence that we have in Him, that if we ask anything according to His will, He hears us. And if we know that He hears us, whatever we ask, we know that we have the petitions that we have asked of Him.

—1 John 5:14–15

Therefore I say to you, whatever things you ask when you pray, believe that you receive them, and you will have them.

—Mark 11:24

"Amen."

NOTES

INTRODUCTION

1. Andrew Murray, *With Christ in the School of Prayer* (London: James Nisbet and Company, 1887), vi–vii. Viewed at Google Books.

PART ONE
THE COURT OF HEAVEN

1. Oswald Chambers, *My Utmost for His Highest: Selections for the Year* (Grand Rapids, MI: Oswald Chambers Publications; Marshall Pickering, 1986), March 7, December 13.

2. Goodreads.com, "Samuel Chadwick Quotes," http://www.goodreads.com/author/quotes/1148687.Samuel_Chadwick (accessed April 22, 2013).

CHAPTER 1
ADVOCACY BEFORE THE THRONE

1. Madame Guyon, *A Short Method of Prayer and Other Writings* (Peabody, MA: Hendrickson Publishers, Inc., 2005), 18.

2. Charles G. Finney, *Lectures on Revivals of Religion* (New York: Leavitt, Lord and Company, 1835), 218. Viewed at Google Books.

3. J. Paul Reno, "Prevailing Prince of Prayer (Daniel Nash)," 1989, http://hopefaithprayer.com/prayernew/prevailing-prince-of-prayer-daniel-nash-j-paul-reno/ (accessed April 22, 2013).

4. As referenced in Leonard Ravenhill, *Why Revival Tarries* (Bloomington, MN: Bethany House, 2004), 53. Viewed at Google Books.

5. Kenneth Hagin, *The Art of Prayer* (Tulsa, OK: Faith Library Publications, 1992), 13.

6. Ibid.

7. Cindy Jacobs, *Possessing the Gates of the Enemy* (Grand Rapids, MI: Chosen Books, 2009), 59. Viewed at Google Books.

8. Dick Eastman, *Love on Its Knees* (Tarrytown, NY: Chosen Books, 1989), 21, as quoted in Jacobs, *Possessing the Gates of the Enemy*, 57. Viewed at Google Books.

9. John Wesley, *A Plain Account of Christian Perfection*, in *The Works of the Rev. John Wesley*, vol. 8 (New York: J. & J. Harper, 1827), 60. Viewed at Google Books.

10. Charles G. Finney, *Memoirs of Rev. Charles G. Finney* (New York: A. S. Barnes and Company, 1876), 142–143. Viewed at Google Books.

CHAPTER 2
THE KING WE SERVE

1. Oswald Chambers, *My Utmost for His Highest* (New York: Dodd, Mead and Company, 1985), March 19.

2. W. E. Vine, Merrill F. Unger, and William White Jr., *Vine's Complete Expository Dictionary of Old and New Testament Words*, vol. 2 (Nashville: Thomas Nelson, 1996), s.v. "peace; shalom."

3. Chambers, *My Utmost for His Highest*, March 20.

CHAPTER 3
DRESSED FOR SUCCESS

1. Edward M. Bounds, *Power Through Prayer* (Chicago: Moody Publishers, 2009), 18. Viewed at Google Books.

2. QuotationsBook.com, *Quotes by Martin Luther* (N.p.: N.d.,), 1. Viewed at Google Books.

3. Andrew Murray, *The Prayer Life* (N.p.: ReadaClassic .com, 2011), 9.

4. Norman Grubb, *Rees Howells, Intercessor* (Fort Washington, PA: CLC Publications, 1952), 83–86. Viewed at Google Books.

5. Chambers, *My Utmost for His Highest*, March 15.

6. D. L. Moody, *Prevailing Prayer: What Hinders It?* (Chicago: Fleming H. Revell, 1884), 102. Viewed at Google Books.

7. Murray, *With Christ in the School of Prayer*, 59–60. Viewed at Google Books.

CHAPTER 4
"WHAT'S NEXT, PAPA?"

1. Bounds, *Power Through Prayer*, 112. Viewed at Google Books.

2. John Wesley, *The Journal of John Wesley*, Christian Classics Ethereal Library, http://www.ccel.org/ccel/wesley/journal.vi.ii.xvi.html (accessed April 24, 2013).

3. Vine, Unger, and White, *Vine's Complete Expository Dictionary of Old and New Testament Words*, s.v. "grace."

4. Charles G. Finney, *Power, Passion, and Prayer* (Alachua, FL: Bridge-Logos, 2004), 177–178. Viewed at Google Books.

5. Wesley, *A Plain Account of Christian Perfection*, 61. Viewed at Google Books.

PART TWO
THE DISCIPLINE OF INTERCESSION

1. Grubb, *Rees Howells, Intercessor*, 212. Viewed at Google Books.

CHAPTER 5
FIRST OF ALL

1. Andrew Murray, *The Ministry of Intercession* (London: James Nisbet and Co., Ltd., 1898), 203. Viewed at Google Books.

2. For more on praying the "disciple's prayer" as an outline for your own Holy Spirit–led prayer times, see my book *The Prayer Warrior's Way*, which goes into much more depth on that subject than we have space to discuss here.

3. *Spider-Man*, directed by Sam Raimi (2002; Hollywood, CA: Columbia Pictures, 2002), DVD.

4. As quoted in H. John Lyke, *What Would Our Founding Fathers Say?* (Bloomington, IN: iUniverse, 2012), 130. Viewed at Google Books.

5. Chambers, *My Utmost for His Highest*, April 1.

CHAPTER 6
BROTHERS AND SISTERS IN CHAINS

1. Andrew Murray, *The Prayer Life* (Chicago: Moody Publishers, 1941), chapter 1. Viewed at Google Books.

2. Susan Llewelyn Leach, "Slavery Is Not Dead, Just Less Recognizable," *Christian Science Monitor*, September 1,

2004, http://www.csmonitor.com/2004/0901/p16s01-wogi
.html (accessed April 25, 2013); Stephanie Hanes, "Human
Trafficking: A Misunderstood Global Scourge," *Christian
Science Monitor,* September 9, 2012, http://www
.csmonitor.com/World/Global-Issues/2012/0909/Human
-trafficking-a-misunderstood-global-scourge (accessed April
25, 2013).

3. Helen Mees, "Does Legalizing Prostitution Work?",
Project Syndicate, February 3, 2009, http://www
.policyinnovations.org/ideas/commentary/data/000107
(accessed April 25, 2013); Rachel Lloyd, "Legality Leads to
More Trafficking," *New York Times,* April 19, 2012, http://
www.nytimes.com/roomfordebate/2012/04/19/is-legalized
-prostitution-safer/legalizing-prostitution-leads-to-more
-trafficking (accessed April 25, 2013).

4. Suzanne Eller, "More Christians Have Been Killed
for Their Faith in the 20th Century Than Have Been Mar-
tyred in the Total History of Christianity," ASSIST News
Service, September 21, 2001, http://www.assistnews.net/
strategic/s0109069.htm (accessed April 25, 2013).

5. UCANews.com, "Persecution Kills 150,000 Christians Every Year," September 12, 2012, http://www
.ucanews.com/news/persecution-kills-150000-christians
-every-year/60090 (accessed April 25, 2013).

6. Shaohua Chen and Martin Ravallion, "The Devel-
oping World Is Poorer Than We Thought, but No Less
Successful in the Fight Against Poverty," World Bank,
August 2008, as referenced in Anup Shah, "Poverty Facts
and Stats," GlobalIssues.org, January 7, 2013, http://www
.globalissues.org/article/26/poverty-facts-and-stats (accessed
April 25, 2013).

7. Anup Shah, "Today, Around 21,000 Children Died Around the World," GlobalIssues.org, September 24, 2011, http://www.globalissues.org/article/715/today-21000 -children-died-around-the-world (accessed April 25, 2013).

8. NBCNews.com. "Today Is World Water Day; More Than 780 Million People Don't Have Access to Clean Water," PHOTOBlog, March 22, 2012, http://photoblog .nbcnews.com/_news/2012/03/22/10813804-today-is-world -water-day-more-than-780-million-people-dont-have-access -to-clean-water?lite (accessed April 25, 2013).

9. Michael Elliott, "Bono: Fight Poverty to 'Zero Zone,'" March 17, 2013, http://www.cnn.com/2013/03/17/opinion/ elliott-bono-ted-poverty (accessed April 25, 2013).

10. World Health Organization, "Malaria: Fact Sheet No. 94," March 2013, http://www.who.int/mediacentre/ factsheets/fs094/en/ (accessed April 25, 2013).

11. E. G. Carre, ed., *Praying Hyde: The Life Story of John Hyde* (Alachua, FL: Bridge Logos, 1982), 32. Viewed at Google Books.

CHAPTER 7
IN WORD AND DEED

1. Vine, Unger, and White, *Vine's Complete Expository Dictionary of Old and New Testament Words*, s.v. "perfect."

2. E. M. Bounds, *The Necessity of Prayer*, chapter 8, "Prayer and Character and Conduct," viewed at Christian Classics Ethereal Library, http://www.ccel.org/ccel/ bounds/necessity.ix.html (accessed April 30, 2013).

3. S. D. Gordon, *Quiet Talks on Prayer* (New York: Fleming H. Revell Company, 1904), 19.

CHAPTER 8
LET JUSTICE ROLL DOWN

1. The following dialogue is taken from Acts 9:4–6.
2. Finney, *Lectures on Revivals of Religion*, 96. Viewed at Google Books.
3. Chambers, *My Utmost for His Highest*, March 31.
4. Prayer based on Ephesians 1:17–19.

APPENDIX B
AN EXAMPLE OF A PRAYER GUIDE FOR PRAYING THE DISCIPLE'S PRAYER

1. See www.whitehouse.gov/administration/cabinet, www.senate.gov, and www.house.gov for names of national government officials.

CindyTrimm.com
Let's stay connected!

CINDY TRIMM

Be sure to visit us online at *CindyTrimm.com* for lots of online resources to empower, equip and encourage you daily!

Videos • Blogs • Articles
Speaking Event Schedule • TV Broadcast Information
Online Resources • Email Subscribe
...and more!

 @cindytrimm

 facebook.com/drtimm

Watch Dr. Cindy's Television Program Weekly

CINDY TRIMM

THE WORD Network

SUNDAYS @ 8AM EST

Be sure to visit us online at *CindyTrimm.com*
for new broadcast times and listings.

Weekly Empowerment Messages in your Email Box!
Subscribe to Dr. Cindy's Free Weekly Email Newsletter
and receive weekly video messages, blogs, and
special announcemnets!

Empowerment
Moments

When you sign up for Empowerment Moments,
you'll receive a fresh word of encouragement
from Dr. Cindy each week!

SIGN UP TODAY!

CindyTrimm.com

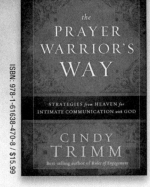
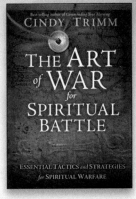

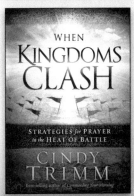